grass scapes

gardening with ornamental grasses

WITHDRAWN

Martin Quinn and Catherine Macleod

 Ball Publishing

Gardens are made by vision, hard physical work, tremendous humility and perpetual learning. This is also true of making books. In the creation of *Grass Scapes* I owe a lot to ornamental grass pioneers like Karl Foerster, Wolfgang Oehme and Kurt Bluemel. I am also grateful to Franz Peters, a fellow grower at Humber Nurseries in Toronto and friend Carolin Brooks, now of Owen Sound, who shared my earliest enthusiasm for ornamental grasses. I learned from authors, landscape architects, designers and educators like Liz Klose and Michael Pascoe, people whose work with ornamental grasses helped transform that early enthusiasm into a passion.

Very personal thanks, however, go to my first teachers, my parents Joyce and Harold Quinn, and to friends in local horticultural societies and Master Gardener groups.

I am grateful to those kind spirits whose interest and encouragement supported me as this book took shape — Lori Bale, Sheila Burr, Guiliana Colalillo, Jim Dalton, Liz Klose, Betty Lamont, Jennifer MacKay, Robby Macleod, Tyler Macleod, Doris Milne, Don Milne, John Melo, Jan Moyser, Vincenzo Pietropaolo and Julie Young. A special thanks goes to visual artist Wendy Hogenbirk for her skill in bringing grasses to life in watercolour. I also want to thank editor Elaine Jones for helping shape our book with patience and knowledge. She is a wizard. The courtly spirit of Robert McCullough and the diplomacy of Robin Rivers have made the creative journey both nurturing and nourishing.

Finally, I am grateful to my co-author and spouse, Catherine Macleod, who helped me find a way to make my grass scapes accessible and who opened that gate with love, faith and trust.

Martin Quinn, Kincardine, Ontario
January 2003

contents

foreword

Liz Klose

From prairie grasslands to meadows, woodlands, roadsides and even lawns, nature dresses the landscape in grasses. This family of plants has long been a staple food and provided shelter for humans and wildlife. More recently, grass has become the primary groundcover in home landscapes. This book, however, goes beyond the boundaries of grass as a green expanse of turf. Gardeners, more than ever before, are turning to ornamental grasses in their landscapes, using them in perennial beds and as sculptural elements and specimens.

This book demystifies grass terminology and reveals the plethora of colours in the ornamental grass palate. You will learn that ornamental grasses are superb companions to bulbs, conifers, shrubs and trees. The perennial companion section highlights just a few perfect partners. By knowing how to design with and care for ornamental grasses you will also discover innovative ideas for incorporating them in the landscape. The "Grasses at a Glance"

section is an especially useful summary.

Whether they are used in bold dramatic sweeps, as groundcovers and screens, or as focal points and container plants, grasses are tremendously versatile in any garden design. Their extended season of interest — from the moment they emerge in the spring to when they punctuate the blanket of snow in winter — adds to their importance as a design element.

Grasses have a linear quality that helps structure the garden. This can take various forms, from graceful fountain-like cascades and tufted mounds to towering open vase shapes and stiff upright spikes. Some grasses evolve through several different textures and forms, resulting in an ever-changing dimension in the garden throughout the growing season.

Grasses are relatively low maintenance; once established they are quite drought tolerant, with some selections performing very well in moist conditions. Most of the grasses detailed here are clump-forming grasses that are well behaved

A true colourist can create harmony with 20 different reds. The reddest of red perennial grasses is *Imperata cylindrica* var. *koenigii* 'Red Baron' (Japanese blood grass). In this rock planting, 'Red Baron' illuminates *Eriophorum angustifolium* (cotton grass) and *Pennisetum alopecuroides* (fountain grass) growing nearby.

in the garden. Some spread slowly by rhizomes and others are more vigorous. The vigorous selections are best suited for ground covers or slope establishment. Essentially there is an ornamental grass for every habitat — naturalized or in a formal garden, in full sun or shade.

Far from being a monochromatic green, grass foliage comes in various hues, tints, and intensities of colour that change with the seasons. The inflorescences also have their own colour, ranging from purple to taupe, gold and eventually wheat.

Rustling and whispering, they lure us into our gardens. The flexible foliage bends and dances in the slightest breeze. Delicate seed heads catch the light. Morning sunlight illuminating dew or frost on the foliage is enchanting, as is the reflection of ornamental grasses nestled along the edge of a pond.

In *Grass Scapes*, Martin and Catherine have captured this magic.

Imperata cylindrica var. **koenigii** 'Red Baron' (Japanese blood grass), **Eriophorum angustifolium** (cotton grass) and **Pennisetum alopecuroides** (fountain grass).

introduction

My mother was working in a flower shop in Guildford, England, during the Second World War when she met my father, a young soldier raised on a Canadian farm. Joyce Martin married Harold Quinn and moved with him to Kincardine, Ontario, where they set up a florist shop and nursery. Their small business in a small town flourished. As children, my sisters and I all helped out. We shared the joy of other families as they prepared for weddings or celebrated births; we also quietly shared their sorrows, delivering flowers of encouragement to hospital nursing stations and flowers of respect to funeral chapels.

My four sisters, Helen, Judy, Susan and Nancy, and I worked in our family greenhouses as far back as I can remember. We planted trees, designed gardens and laid sod. We seeded, divided and propagated. In travels all over the province with our father, we met and chatted with almost everyone who worked in the horticultural industry. My favourite task, however, was working

in the enchanting gardens of gentle "ladies," who served me lemonade after the weeding, transplanting, grass cutting or trimming was done. When I finished high school I studied horticulture at Algonquin College in Ottawa and have worked in the industry ever since.

My interest in ornamental grasses began during a horticultural trip to England, Holland and Germany in 1985. At that time I became aware of the pioneering work of German horticulturist and perennial hybridizer Karl Foerster.

In Europe I saw ornamental grasses growing in climatic conditions very similar to those I knew in Canada and the northern U.S. I decided to test the common wisdom of the day and find out if they were hardy enough for Canada.

At the time I knew of no one growing ornamental grasses in Canada and had little information to help me select appropriate varieties (later I learned that Franz Peters at Humber Nurseries in Brampton was also interested in

ornamental grasses). I began by importing and working with 85 grasses. This was before the electronic revolution that has made speedy online research possible, so it took me some time to discover that the same ornamental grass bug that had bitten Franz and I had also bitten three people in the U.S.

Kurt Bluemel, the acknowledged driving force behind the Ornamental Grass Movement in North America, had been working with grasses since the 1960s, when, as a student, he encountered their widespread use in Germany and Switzerland. When he moved to the U.S. his designs attracted attention in the Baltimore area, where he settled and opened a nursery.

Ornamental grasses were pushed further into the North American spotlight when landscape architect Wolfgang Oehme — a former Foerster student and Maryland neighbour of Bluemel — teamed up with Dutch-trained Jim Van Sweden. Oehme and Van Sweden used predominantly ornamental grasses in

What is an ornamental grass?

The term "ornamental grass" is used very loosely. "True" grasses are members of the Poaceae family, which includes woody-stemmed bamboos. The other grass-like families are sedges (Cyperaceae), rushes (Juncaceae), restios (Restionaceae) and cattails (Typhaceae). Often sedges, rushes, restios and cattails are lumped in with true grasses when discussing ornamental grasses.

There are also a number of grass-like plants. For example, mondo grass (*Ophiopogon planiscapus*) looks like a grass and its common name makes it sound like a grass, but it is actually a dramatic lookalike that is not a grass at all.

Perennial grasses live and grow for decades. Annual grasses emerge from seed, grow, flower and die in one season. Some plants can be perennial in one climate and annual in another. In our gardens and this book, we focus on hardy ornamental grasses and sedges.

Although bamboo is actually one of the largest and oldest members of the Poaceae family, for now we use these manificent perennials primarily as companions to the other grasses we grow. Evergreen bamboos bring animation and an exotic look to the garden scene and are quickly earning a place in North American gardens.

introduction

the redesign of the Federal Reserve Building in Washington, D.C. in 1977, sparking a horticultural revolution in the U.S.

In 1991 I met Michael Pascoe, Chief Horticulturist at the Cuddy Garden in Strathroy, Ontario, and he introduced me to Liz Klose of the School of Horticulture at Niagara Parks Botanical Gardens in Niagara Falls. She was undertaking a dramatic expansion of the grass gardens there. Liz called me about potential selections and I was happy to supply her with some new acquisitions.

In our own hardiness testing, in Strathroy first and now in our Kincardine greenhouses, we discovered that a number of varieties for Zone 7 would actually grow in Zone 4. I was heartened when Agriculture and Agri-Food Canada published the results of its intensive evaluation of 160 grasses in over 80 species and 43 genera for the Northern Great Plains. Authors Davidson and Gobin at the Morden Research Centre in Manitoba provided

the scientific evidence that proved there is indeed a wide range of low-maintenance grasses hardy enough to grow in cold and generally dry conditions. Ornamental grasses now enjoy one of the top perennial spots in the "best cultivar" charts of the Michigan State University annual floriculture industry survey. Although the Canadian industry does not yet conduct its own study, nurseries are experiencing the positive impact of the ornamental grass movement in Canadian gardening.

When I realized that local gardeners working in small spaces were hesitant to use ornamental grasses because of their heights — some more than 6 feet (1.8 m), I began to hybridize shorter grasses suitable for Ontario conditions. (This doesn't mean I don't recommend the tall grasses for a small garden, because I do and will continue to promote them as important specimen plants in even the smallest of spaces.)

Our first successes were *Miscanthus sinensis* 'Huron Sunrise' and 'Huron

Sunset.' They are unique for their flower colour — a deep burgundy, much darker than any of the other *Miscanthus* species available — and for their relatively low height. 'Huron Sunrise' grows to 4 feet (120 cm) and 'Huron Sunset' reaches 3 feet (90 cm).

'Huron Sunrise' and 'Huron Sunset' now thrive in our one-acre (.4-hectare) demonstration gardens. They grow in clay soil on land that for years served as stony fields for cattle. To the original barns and sheds we have added a number of hoop greenhouses as we have made the horticultural transition to a low-tech, family operation. What our demonstration gardens may lack in formal design unity they make up for in the variety of unique and challenging beds we are developing in shade, full sun, dry and wet conditions. Many of the 120 varieties of grass we now grow play significant and varied roles in these beds and perennial borders.

The new prominence of grasses in garden design is one small step in a long history of ornamental and practical plant-growing that goes back millenia.

North American gardening history began thousands of years ago when aboriginal people broke soil to plant vegetable seeds, gathered wild rice or processed cereal grain grasses like corn, wheat, rye or oats for sustenance. Other lovely grasses, like bamboo, played practical roles in early construction as well as ornamental roles in Chinese and Japanese garden art.

Ornamental grasses were somewhat popular in the early years of the twentieth century in North America, but by the 1940s they had fallen into a state of sad cliché in the over-present pampas grasses of suburban landscapes. It wasn't until plant breeders and designers like Karl Foerster, Kurt Bluemel, Wolfgang Oehme, Jim Van Sweden and Piet Oudolf came on the scene that ornamental grasses regained prominence. In a move away from the old horticultural

introduction

schools of mastery and imitation and toward gardening in harmony with nature, this group has established its own natural school of design. They have also placed grass gardening squarely in the heart of today's environmental movement.

Although gardening in a natural style has never been easier than it is with perennial ornamental grasses, they are still relatively unknown. Many garden centres carry somewhat limited selections and when these are displayed beside other bedding plants or perennials the withered-looking shoots of potted baby grasses can sometimes look like ugly ducklings.

Remarkably adaptable and resilient, however, they prove to be hardy, relatively disease and pest free and very low maintenance. Most thrive in the sun, but they flourish in a wide range of light, soil, climate and moisture conditions. Now that these traits are better known, ornamental grasses are being planted in public and private gardens,

golf courses and parks. They are recognized for their beauty and ability to attract butterflies and birds. And they are also being pressed into environmental service in large-scale erosion control, water purification and naturalizing projects.

When Catherine and I married in 1991 we started the grass business and began planning to move home to Kincardine where our parents, families and many dear old friends lived.

In our dream was an old home on land with some character, a few acres for greenhouses, some sturdy outbuildings and room for offices and a classroom. In 1997 we bought that farm. Our plans didn't include writing a book on gardening with ornamental grasses, but it became obvious that with my photographs and practical knowledge and Catherine's writing skills we had everything we needed to produce *Grass Scapes*. In the summer of 2000 we rolled up our sleeves and started

to work on it in earnest.

Grass Scapes is an introduction to gardening with hardy ornamental grasses. It is written for gardeners at all levels of practice and shows how a simple understanding of basic grass shapes, sizes, colours and functions can open the door to gardening confidently with hardy ornamental grasses. We hope you will use it to bring these beautiful, versatile and useful plants into your own gardens and communities.

Hardiness Zones

In grass hardiness tests we have found that a number of Zone 7 varieties grow well in Zone 4 if there is good snow cover. Grasses identified as Zone 7 plants grow easily into Zone 6 and sometimes right into Zone 4 when deep snow cover protects the ground from frost. Keep in mind that zone ratings are not always a perfect gauge for determining winter hardiness. In some southern locations a particular plant may die in winter while the same variety, snug under a blanket of snow, may be fine farther north.

Gardeners in Canada and the U.S. can refer to their appropriate Hardiness Zone Maps, which are based on average climatic conditions of each area. These take into account minimum winter temperatures, length of the frost-free period, summer rainfall, maximum temperatures, snow cover, January rainfall and maximum wind speed.

Although the Canadian and U.S. maps overlap some-what, they are not the same. The Canadian map has nine zones — from the Yukon to temperate B.C. The U.S. map has 11 zones, ranging from Alaska to tropical Hawaii. The recent Agriculture Canada map also includes significant subzones and incorporates the impact of elevation — especially important in western Canada and the US. Readers who have access to the Internet can visit the Web site. Each site is hyperlinked so that visitors can type the name of their community and zoom into excellent close-ups.

These maps offer a guideline, but year-to-year variations in weather and gardening techniques can impact on plant survival in any particular location. Wise gardeners, therefore, still rely on local gardening expertise and word of mouth — as we have since the beginning of gardening time.

Canada   http://sis.agr.gc.ca/cansis/nsdb/climate/hardiness/intro.html
U.S.   http://www.usna.usda.gov/Hardzone/ushzmap.html

about grasses

Ornamental grasses challenge some of the traditional approaches to garden design, but they bring a new sense of life and drama to the garden. Perhaps their most exceptional quality — the one that cannot be drawn onto any plan or illustrated on any garden centre tag — is animation. Even the most subtle of breezes will create a virtual ballet of movement and sound. Grasses in motion can whisper like silk, rustle like satin, whistle like wind or wail like a winter storm.

Playfulness with light is another outstanding attribute.
From dawn to dusk, the changing light transforms a grass
garden's character, mood and form — intensifying
foliage and flower shape, heightening colour or tossing
the grasses into dramatic silhouette.

The first step in using grasses is to become familiar with
how they grow — from their roots to their flowers — and
how to care for them.

root systems and growth habit

True ornamental grasses have two distinct growing habits — clump-forming and spreading.

clumpers

Clumpers grow in lateral shoots from their base, keeping the plant compact. They are slow, steady growers and these grasses are the ones used most in beds and borders as accents, in mosaic plantings, for layering or in mass plantings.

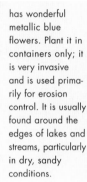

**Leymus
arenarius glauca**
(blue lime grass)

runners

Runners, or spreading grasses, spread
by above-ground horizontal roots called
stolons, which can produce new plants
at each node or by underground rhizomes. Some grasses with aggressive
spreading root systems, like *Spartina
pectinata* (prairie cord grass) and
Phalaris arundinacea (ribbon grass), can
vary from highly invasive to moderately
invasive and may be used successfully
with a bit of attention and special care.

Many people are put off when they
know that a grass has a spreading habit,
but invasive grasses play important
roles in bank establishment and erosion
control. They can be used in a garden
setting if they are kept in check with an
attentive eye and a good sharp spade or
as container plants.

has wonderful
metallic blue
flowers. Plant it in
containers only; it
is very invasive
and is used prima-
rily for erosion
control. It is usually
found around the
edges of lakes and
streams, particularly
in dry, sandy
conditions.

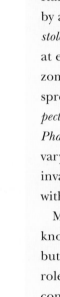

leaves, stems and flowers

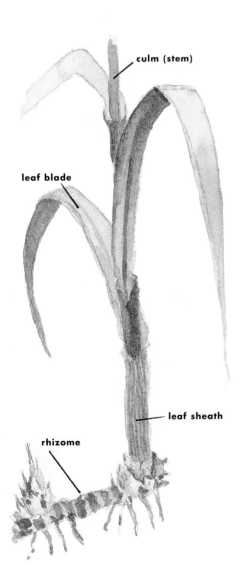

culm (stem)

leaf blade

leaf sheath

rhizome

leaves

Each leaf is composed of three parts —
a vertical *sheath*, which grows from a
node and wraps around the stem; an
almost invisible *ligule*, which is a pro-
tective membrane of thin hairs at the
juncture of the sheath; and a *blade*, the
part of the leaf above the sheath.

The grass blade grows away from
the stem and is usually open and narrow
with parallel veins and a large median
vein called a *midrib*. *Miscanthus sinensis*
leaves range in width from $1/4$ to $1/2$ inch
(.6 to 1.2 cm) and have a distinctive and
prominent white midrib. The overall
height of a grass does not necessarily
determine the size of the leaves: the
bold, glossy leaves of *Hakonechloa macra*
(hakone grass) are the same width as
those of the very tall *M. sinensis*
'Gracillimus' (maiden grass).

Grass has an unusual way of growing
that contributes to its survival. Most
plants grow from the tips of their leaves

Chasmanthium latifolium

and branches. Anyone who has cared for a lawn will know that grass has two distinct growing points — at the base of each leaf and just above each growth node on the stem. This growth pattern means that grass can keep on growing even after cutting, cropping by animals, or even fire.

stems

Most grass stems, or *culms,* are herbaceous, hollow and cylindrical or slightly flattened. The rounded shape is one way to differentiate them from sedges, most of which have three-angled stems. (The stems of sedges are also pithy, not hollow like grasses.) The leaves are attached at swollen joints called nodes. The *internode* is the stem part between the nodes.

alamagrotsis x **acutiflora** 'Karl Foerster'

flowers

What we call grass flowers are actually a complex group of structures, usually arranged in clusters on a stem, which together are called an *inflorescence.* The three basic flower types of grass flowers are a *spike,* a *raceme* and a *panicle.*

inflorescence

A *spike* is elongated; the individual spikelets have no stalks and are attached directly to the central axis or *rachis.* *Pennisetum setaceum* 'Rubrum' (red fountain grass) is an example.

A *raceme* is more open; the spikelets are suspended from the *rachis* on short stalks. An example is *Chasmanthium latifolium* (northern sea oats), with tiny, oat-like stems.

spikelet   **floret**

pike *Pennisetum setaceum* 'Rubrum' (red fountain grass)
nd *Alopecurus pratensis* (yellow foxtail)

raceme *Phalaris arundinacea* (ribbon grass) and
Chasmanthium latifolium (northern sea oats)

flowers (continued)

A *panicle* is multi-branched and very open; stalks branch out from the rachis and stemmed spikelets are attached to these stalks. *Deschampsia cespitosa* (tufted hair grass) is an example.

Some flowers are a compound of panicles and racemes. Together panicles and racemes create the magnificent plumes of *Miscanthus sinensis* flowers.

Awns are slender, often silky, sometimes stiff bristles attached to the bract of a grass flower. Awns create the beautiful plumes on grasses like *Hordeum jubatum*.

panicle *Bromus inermis* (smooth brome)

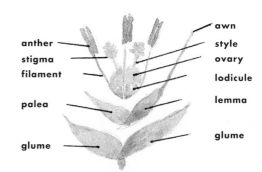

anther
stigma
filament
palea
glume

awn
style
ovary
lodicule
lemma
glume

compound of panicles and racemes
Miscanthus sinensis

Miscanthus sinensis 'Sarabande'

grass forms

For our purposes we divide grasses into six general structures: upright, upright arching, arching, upright divergent, mounded and tufted.

upright

grasses come in a variety of heights, but tall, medium or small, they all provide linear exclamation points in a garden design. The foliage and flowers of the medium-high *Calamagrostis arundinacea* var. *brachytricha* (fall-blooming reed grass) grows from a tidy clumping base of 30 inches to 3 feet (75 to 90 cm) in flower. Arrow-straight, with upright vertical leaves and erect, slender flower heads, it works equally well as an individual specimen or in mass plantings. *Imperata cylindrica* 'Red Baron' (Japanese blood grass) is small at 16 inches (40 cm), but this intensely red decorative is another popular upright grass.

A six-year-old *Calamagrostis* 'Overdam'. This grass is hardy, very erect and sturdy. It has a vigorous clumping habit and grows to about 30 inches (75 cm) in height. The leaves are about 1/2 inch (1.2 cm) wide. Flowers are pink, turning blonde by September. 'Overdam' is a good companion plant for *Miscanthus floridulus* or the amazing red *Panicum* 'Warrior.'

Calamagrostis x **acutiflora 'Overdam'**

upright **upright arching**

upright arching

foliage springs from the base, ascends stiffly and vertically, then falls in a fountain of arcs from the top. The low-growing burgundy annual *Pennisetum setaceum* 'Eaton Canyon' (miniature red fountain grass) with bottlebrush-like flowers, *Molinia caerulea* 'Variegata' (variegated moor grass) and the statuesque *Saccharum ravennae* (hardy pampas grass) are all good examples. *Arundo donax* (Giant reed) and *Chasmanthium latifolium* (northern sea oats) are two of the tallest grass varieties. In full flower, magnificent *C. latifolium* flower heads droop languidly well above their foliage.

Native to wet prairies and marshes from Maine to the great plains, the tall variegated *Spartina pectinata* 'Aureomarginata' (prairie cord grass) is stately, upright and arching. Its golden flowers in late July or early August look great near ponds.

Miscanthus sinensis 'Gracillimus'
accenting a garden bench in a small townhouse garden

Hordeum jubatum
(foxtail barley)

arching

varieties include the popular *Miscanthus sinensis,* which has over 60 named cultivars, each charming in its own way. *M. sinensis* foliage grows vertically at slight angles from its clumping base; an outstanding example is 'Huron Sentinel' (Huron Sentinel maiden grass). This new introduction is a superb specimen in a bed or border. Alone it is like a solitary royal guardsman; in a mass planting, it is like an entire regiment at attention.

The beautifully arching *Hordeum jubatum* (foxtail barley) grows to 18 inches (45 cm) high and 2 feet (60 cm) wide at maturity, with a purplish flower. It makes a good naturalizing plant as its seed is viable and grows easily. *Lupine* and *Penstemon grandiflorus* (beard-tongue) are good companions.

upright divergent

upright divergent

foliage grows up and out from its base at a forty-degree angle in a stiffly vertical manner, like a slightly open fan. The multi-purpose beauty *Calamagrostis* x *acutiflora* 'Karl Foerster' (feather reed grass) is a fine example. The stately native prairie variety *Andropogon gerardii* (big bluestem) is another.

Spectacular *Molinia caerulea* ssp. *arundinacea* 'Skyracer' in flower can be up to 8 feet (2.4 m) high from a base clump of about 3 feet (90 cm) at ground level. In late autumn its leaves are a rich golden yellow. The delicate panicles appear in July in glorious sprays of rich purple or bronze. In autumn, the flower matures to a subtle blonde. 'Skyracer' has a strong yet graceful sculptural form and lasts for years with minimal maintenance. It grows best in full sun with plenty of moisture but will tolerate dry conditions as well.

Molinia caerulea ssp. **arundinacea** 'Skyracer'

mounded

mounded

grass forms have foliage that cascades over lower leaves. They are generally small to medium in height. There are relatively few varieties that take this form, but mounded grasses are good choices for adding texture, punctuating beds and creating borders. Good decorative grasses are *Hakonechloa macra* 'Aureola' (golden variegated hakone grass) and *Helictotrichon sempervirens* (blue oat grass). Mounded varieties are great companions for taller grasses because they can be used effectively to cover the unsightly "bare legs" that often appear at the base of taller varieties as a season progresses.

Carex muskingumensis (palm sedge), a North America native, grows in sunny areas and dappled shade to a height of 2 feet (60 cm). It needs moist soil. Good bog garden companion plants are *Eupatorium maculatum* (joe pye weed) and *Eupatorium perfoliatum* (boneset).

Carex muskingumensis (palm sedge)

**Festuca
amethystina**
'Superba'

tufted

grasses have short, thin and spiky
upright leaves. There are relatively few
named varieties that take this form.
Two examples are fine-textured grasses
like the small *Festuca glauca* 'Boulder
Blue' (blue fescue) and *Deschampsia
cespitosa* (tufted hair grass). *Festuca
amethystina* 'Superba' has lovely, rainbow-
coloured flower stems above bright
blue leaves.

The tufted *Helictotrichon sempervirens* (blue oat
grass) pictured here in the right foreground has
been a best-selling perennial grass for a number
of years. Very compact, with a striking metallic
blue colour, this versatile plant grows to about
16 inches (40 cm) across and 2 feet (60 cm)
high with a 46-inch (1.2-m) flower height. It
prospers in all conditions, from dry to wet and
sun to shade. Its fine texture complements many
different plants. In the garden we like the contrast
of brown-leafed *Eupatorium* 'Chocolate' or
heavily textured *Sedum* 'Autumn Joy.'

Helictotrichon sempervirens (blue oat grass)

how grasses are named

All plants have botanical names, and these are the standard for identification.

Miscanthus sinensis 'Huron Sunrise'

They help alleviate confusion that can be caused by the many common names that inevitably attach themselves to well-loved plants. When I write about grasses I place the common name, which is usually the easiest to remember, in brackets after the botanical name. Botanical names have two basic parts: the *genus* and the *species*. The genus represents a number of species sharing distinctive characteristics and is always capitalized and in italics. The species name is also in italics but is not capitalized. (Note that the plural of genus is "genera" and that in some horticultural texts you may run into the term "specific epithet" for species.)

In nature there are many minor variations within species and these can be designated by subspecies or varieties (abbreviated as ssp. and var.). These terms are not italicized.

Breeders cultivate specific characteristics in grasses and these are called cultivars (shortened from cultivated variety) and given names that are enclosed in single quotation marks.

Molinia caerulea ssp. **arundinacea** 'Skyracer'

The chart below compares *Miscanthus sinensis* and *Molinia caerulea.*

Plant Name	*Miscanthus sinensis* 'Huron Sunrise'	*Molinia caerulea* ssp. *arundinacea* 'Skyracer'
Genus	*Miscanthus*	*Molinia*
Species (or specific epithet)	*sinensis*	*caerulea*
Variety or subspecies	N/A	*arundinacea*
Cultivar	'Huron Sunrise'	'Skyracer'
Common name	(Huron silver grass)	(Tall purple moor grass)

cultivation and maintenance

Ornamental grasses thrive in the kind of soils found in most gardens — a combination of clay and sand amended with perculite, vermiculite and humus obtained from grass or leaf mulch, peat moss, straw and compost.

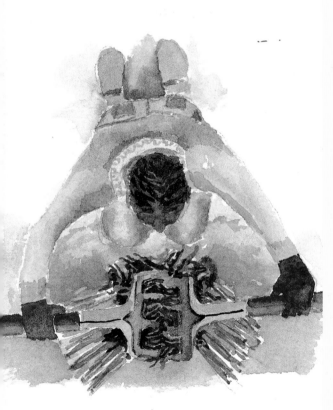

Grasses do not require high fertility and adapt well to all soil conditions, from sand to heavy clay. In clay they usually take an extra year to mature. In sandy soil, with less moisture, they tend to be smaller in height.

The efficient fibrous root systems of grasses make them especially drought-resistant. Occasionally, in very wet seasons, grass foliage can succumb to rust, but that problem is easily solved by giving the plants more space and breathing room. Ornamental grasses provide all-season interest except during the few weeks in spring when we trim them. Then borders and beds look polka-dotted with giant pincushions. This prickly phenomenon lasts only two or three weeks as new shoots begin to appear almost immediately. It's a good diversionary tactic to cut grasses back when their colourful spring bulb neigh-bours are in bloom.

Grasses are either warm- or cool-season species, depending on their periods of active growth. Warm-season

grasses, like *Miscanthus sinensis,* grow roots in warm weather. Cool-season grasses like *Holcus mollis* grow roots in spring and autumn and sleep during hot weather.

dividing grasses

The grasses covered in this book are mostly perennials, so treat them as you do all others — divide them when they are too large or when the centres die out and become unsightly.

In cooler climates it is best to divide plants in the spring. We keep it simple by doing all the dividing in spring. Most climatic zones do not have a long enough growing season for warm-season grasses — those that thrive in fine weather — to root properly before the onset of winter if divided in autumn.

When dividing grasses, dig around the plant with a shovel or spade about 6 inches (15 cm) away from the clump. Then dig under the clump and lift it out of the hole. Plunge two digging forks, back to back, into the root ball.

dividing grasses dig around the plant with a shovel or spade about 6 inches (15 cm) away from the clump.

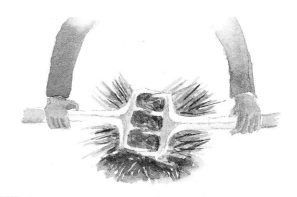

dividing grasses (continued)

Some mature clumps require a good jump on the forks in order to penetrate the root mass. Depending on the size of the plant and allowing for a 4-inch (20-cm) root mass in each new division, you can make two, four or eight plants.

dividing tips

- Inspect large grass plants in fall to select grasses for division.

- Divide both warm- and cool-season grasses in spring to keep it simple.

- Use sharp, strong shovels, spades and digging forks.

- Wear good footwear.

- Don't be timid about dividing the roots. Grasses can take it.

- Don't dig any closer than 6 inches (15 cm) from a clump.

- Dig under the root mass, rather than trying to pry the root ball upwards. This could break your spade and shovel handles.

- Plant new divisions immediately, using the guidelines in the planting section. Roots should never be exposed to the sun.

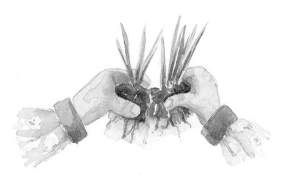

Gently spread the roots apart.

planting grasses

Ornamental grasses can be purchased in garden centres, box stores or through mail-order nurseries that specialize in grasses. Normally they are sold in 5-gallon (20 L), 2- gallon (8 L) or 1-gallon (4 L) (the most popular) sizes. Some mail-order nurseries sell bare-root clumps.

Before planting, do your research. It is important to know the size of ornamental grasses at maturity. Some can grow into giants. Know your site and make sure the new plant you choose is suited to the location. Though exceptions exist, there are general guidelines for spacing. Small grasses need 1 square foot (.09 m²) of room to grow; medium grasses may require 2 to 3 square feet (.18 to .27 m²), depending on the actual height. Tall grasses should have lots of room — 4 square feet (.36 m²) for giants like *Arundo donax*.

ace the grass in the prepared hole and half-fill the hole with soil.

cutting back

Since we enjoy our grasses throughout winter and we like to spread the gardening workload, we don't cut them back until early spring. Spring varies from area to area, so monitor the grasses and cut them back before new growth starts.

planting tips

- Plant in spring, even though some grass varieties will not yet be starting to grow.
- Water the plant well before planting.
- Dig an area three times larger than the size of the pot.
- Amend the soil with peat moss, manure or compost if necessary.
- Remove the plant from the pot. If the root mass fills the pot completely, gently spread the roots apart.
- Place the grass in the prepared hole and half-fill the hole with soil.
- Water well.
- Fill the hole with soil and compress with your hands.
- Be sure the crown is at or just above soil level.
- Don't baby new grasses by overwatering or overfeeding. (They are tough.)

We use a very simple formula to determine how much to cut back. If a grass grows under 3 feet (90 cm) in height, cut it back to 2 inches (5 cm); if a grass grows over 3 feet (90 cm) cut it cut back to 4 inches (10 cm).

We have tried many tools for cutting back — pruners, hedge clippers, electric hedge clippers and weed whippers. We finally settled on a gas-powered hedge trimmer because of the number of plants we grow. Choose the tool that best suits your needs.

In the past we removed grass clippings to the compost heap, but recently we have started to leave the clippings right in the beds. We turn them into mulch by cutting the stalks into sections, snipping the stems off 6 inches (15 cm) at a time until we reach the desired height.

tips for cutting back

- Cut grasses back in early spring, before new growth starts.

- Use newly sharpened and oiled tools.

- Don't be afraid to cut grasses back aggressively. Cut those less than 3 feet (90 cm) back to 2 inches (5 cm) and those over 3 feet (90 cm) back to 4 inches (10 cm)

- Mulch or compost leaves and stems.

- Never cut new growth.

working with colour

One of the first prints we had framed when we started working with ornamental grasses was *The Tangled Garden* by Canadian Group of Seven painter J.E.H. MacDonald (1873–1932). It still hangs above the fireplace in the main room of our house, reminding us of the challenges of the work and, in amber, green and red, complementing the colourful grass gardens visible from the two large windows.

Visual artists and artisans have turned to nature for their colour inspiration and dyes for centuries. Colour can express a mood, provide a background, act as an accent, suggest harmony, give a sense of scale and create the illusion of space and perspective. In a famous 1846 essay, the French poet Baudelaire claimed that nature couldn't make a mistake when it comes to colour because form and colour in nature are one. He believed that true

colourists couldn't make mistakes either, because they seem to know by instinct the tone values, the results of mixing and the science of counterpoint. "That's why they can create harmony with 20 different reds," he explained.

The key word in ornamental grass colour is subtlety. In spring and summer, grasses usually play supporting roles behind more showy shrubs, perennials and annuals. To the uninitiated they may seem like the supporting cast for peonies, roses, delphiniums and other divas. Experienced ornamental grass gardeners, however, know that grass colours range from greens, blues, reds, yellows and browns to white and even black. Variegated grasses are adorned with whites, ivories and creams. The spring and summer garden may have a vibrant colour chorus of funky, lime green *Carex albula* 'Frosty Curls,' a powdery blue *Helictotrichon sempervirens*, an intense burgundy *Pennisetum setaceum* 'Rubrum,' a burgundy

Panicum virgatum 'Huron Solstice,' and a polished bronze *Carex buchananii*. Not only that, but leaves, stems, foliage, seed heads and flower heads can all be different colours. Grasses like *Festuca amethystina*, for example, change dramatically through the season. Its stem is as important as the leaf and flower head in colour selection.

When the summer garden relaxes into autumn, grasses really come into their own. Flower heads are a parade of feathery bonnets and tasseled caps in purples, burgundies, pinks, bronzes, coppers and silvers. Once open and primed to disperse, the seeds take on a subtler but no less dazzling range of hues — gossamer blondes, ethereal golds and diaphanous platinums. A group planting of burgundy-flowered *Miscanthus sinensis* 'Huron Sunrise,' *Panicum virgatum* 'Heavy Metal' and variegated varieties like *Molina caerulea* 'Variegata' can really shine as the days shorten and the quality of light changes.

green   blue   red   pink

A fabulous combination is *Saccharum ravennae* with its towering, spear-like flowers, a medium-sized *Miscanthus sinensis* 'Huron Sunrise' and a small *Deschampsia cespitosa*, which, when in flower, wears a halo of the finest lace. To complete the picture add autumn lingerers like *Athyrium niponicum* 'Pictum' (Japanese painted fern), *Eupatorium rugosum* 'Chocolate,' delphiniums and unbridled cosmos. Almost any grass will dance with a dowager *Rudbeckia* 'Lacinata' or hardy chrysanthemums in autumn. This is also the time when the almost purple *Chasmanthium latifolium*, burgundy *Imperata cylindrica* 'Red Baron' and pink-suffused *Miscanthus sinensis* 'Huron Sunrise' form a vibrant trio. In autumn a crimson *M.* 'Purpurascens' creates a magnificent counterpoint to the golden yellows of *Pennisetum alopecuroides* and *P. alopecuroides* 'Hameln.'

Though it may seem daunting at first, with some practice and observation designing with the colour subtleties of ornamental grasses can be as rewarding as any other artistic or decorative endeavour. The "Grasses at a Glance" section at the back of this book, which profiles over a hundred hardy varieties, will help, for the variations are countless. Whether it is several grasses of one colour in a monochromatic scheme, a dominant colour with a range of complementary colours, or a selection of harmonizers like blues, reds and yellows, ornamental grasses are a colourist's dream.

red (variegated)   bright yellow   bronze   red

summer colour

white variegated

A very young, low-growing *Holcus mollis* 'Albo-variegatus.' Although this small grass looks somewhat like the more sparsely structured *Arrhenatherum elatius* 'Variegatus' (bulbous oat grass), it is not used much in garden design yet. 'Albo-variegatus' is a great ground cover. It mats out first thing in the spring and maintains fullness through-out the growing season if in a shaded area with cool temperatures. It fades away and almost seems to die in too much sun, but as soon as the weather cools downs it bounces back. It grows to only 6 inches (15 cm) in height but in two to three years it spreads to about 1 foot (30 cm).

more summer whites

Arrhenatherum elatius ssp. *bulbosum* 'Variegatus'
Arundo donax 'Variegata'
Calamagrostis x *acutiflora* 'Overdam'
Miscanthus sinensis 'Cabaret'
Miscanthus sinensis 'Morning Light'
Miscanthus sinensis 'Variegatus'
Pennisetum alopecuroides 'Little Honey'
Phalaris arundinacea 'Picta'

white *Holcus mollis* 'Albo-variegatus'

yellow

This vivid *Carex elata* 'Bowles' Golden' with intense yellow foliage adds a pleasing upright structure to any garden. It is relatively slow growing, but given rich, well-drained soil that is high in organic matter it will grow more quickly and display more luxuriant foliage. It performs in a range of conditions, from partial sun to shade. About 18" (45 cm) high, a mature clump can be 1 foot (30 cm) wide.

more summer yellows

Alopecurus pratensis 'Aureus'
Hakonechloa macra 'Aureola'
Miscanthus sinensis 'Huron Penetangore'
Miscanthus sinensis 'Little Zebra'
Miscanthus sinensis 'Puenktchen'
Miscanthus sinensis 'Strictus'
Miscanthus sinensis 'Zebrinus'
Molinia caerulea 'Variegata'

yellow *Carex elata* 'Bowles' Golden' planted with *Artemisia* 'Silver Brocade' and *Ophiopogon planiscapus* 'Niger.' This young planting shows an attractive yellow, silver and black combination.

summer colour

green *Miscanthus sinensis 'Huron Sentinel'*

green

Miscanthus sinensis 'Huron Sentinel' flowers appear in September, bringing the overall height to 5 feet (1.5 m). As the season advances the plumes change from red to deep bronze. When late summer and autumn winds play, it performs a stunning dance number with an equally tall-growing *Rudbeckia* 'Laciniata.' *Panicum virgatum* planted in front creates a pleasing layered effect.

more summer greens

Calamagrostis x *acutiflora* 'Karl Foerster'

Miscanthus sinensis 'Huron Blush'

Miscanthus sinensis 'Huron Sunrise'

Miscanthus sinensis 'Huron Sunset'

Pennisetum alopecuroides 'Little Bunny'

Pennisetum alopecuroides 'Moudry'

Saccharum ravennae

summer colour

blue

A recent introduction, powder blue *Festuca glauca* 'Boulder Blue' is about the same size as *F. glauca* 'Sea Urchin,' although it doesn't flower as well. It is a real eye-catcher, however, when planted with *Carex buchananii* (bronze leather leaf sedge) and *Sedum* 'Vera Jameson.' 'Boulder Blue' tolerates very dry conditions and thrives in heavy or light soil.

more summer blues

Festuca glauca 'Boulder Blue'
Festuca glauca 'Elijah Blue'
Festuca glauca 'Sea Urchin'
Helictotrichon sempervirens
Koeleria glauca
Panicum virgatum 'Heavy Metal'
Panicum virgatum 'Prairie Sky'

Blue *Festuca glauca* 'Boulder Blue'

red

The vibrant red of this translucent, light-rooted *Imperata cylindrica* 'Red Baron' intensifies gradually until the first heavy frosts, when it turns brown. It will grow in partial shade but for the best colour performance it needs full sun in protected spots near rocks.

For astounding contrast try *Imperata cylindrica* 'Red Baron' with *Lamium* 'White Nancy.'

more summer reds
Panicum virgatum 'Shenandoah'
Pennisetum setaceum 'Rubrum'

red *Imperata cylindrica* 'Red Baron'

autumn colour

pink (variegated)

More autumn pinks
Phalaris arundinacea 'Feesey's Form'
Miscanthus sinensis 'Variegatus'
Miscanthus sinensis 'Cabaret'

pink *Phalaris arundinacea* 'Feesey's Form' with Iris in an Edmonton garden.

red

A large stand of about 100 *Miscanthus* 'Purpurascens' (flame grass) in Kitchener, Ontario. 'Purpurascens' gets its name from its autumn foliage colour. It was selected by German nurseryman Dr. Hans Simon in the 1960s and has since proved to have the most reliable red-orange autumn colour of any *Miscanthus* species grown in Canada. The handsome, silver white, compact flower heads are more erect than most *Miscanthus* species and in Ontario appear relatively early, in late August or early September. Just over 5 feet (1.5 metres) tall to the tops of the flowers, its relatively small stature makes it ideal for use in more intimate gardens. A planting of three of these grasses in a smaller garden makes a great backdrop for *Rudbeckia fulgida* 'Goldsturm.'

more autumn reds

Imperata cylindrica 'Red Baron'
Panicum virgatum 'Heavy Metal'
Panicum virgatum 'Warrior'

ed *Miscanthus* 'Purpurascens'

autumn colour

red (variegated)

Hakonechloa macra (hakone forest grass) at its elegant best under a cedar tree in our garden. Its arching bamboo-like leaves are a lovely bronze in autumn. It grows to 1 foot (30 cm) high and 2 feet (60 cm) wide. A versatile groundcover, it resembles rolling waves when animated by wind. Plant it under a leaf canopy of *Hosta* for a lovely layered structure. *H. macra* flourishes in shaded areas in moist or dry conditions.

more autumn reds

Hakonechloa macra 'Aureola'
Panicum virgatum 'Rehbraun'

Red (Variegated) *Hakonechloa macra* (hakone forest grass)

bright yellow

A graceful *Chasmanthium latifolium* (northern sea oats). Clump-forming and upright, it grows from 4 to 5 feet (1.2 to 1.5 m) in height. It is one of the few varieties we grow that produces viable seed. The seeds germinate where they fall and are easily identified when they start growing in very early spring. *C. latifolium* is especially interesting because it has two colour phases in autumn. Its yellow oat-like flower heads, which look like flattened, one-sided silk tassels, bow elegantly from arching terminal branches throughout the season. The yellow foliage, however, turns purple with frost. Plant this fine-leafed grass near a large-leafed hydrangea for a spectacular autumn effect.

More autumn yellows

Molinia caerulea ssp. *arundinacea* 'Skyracer'
Panicum virgatum
Pennisetum alopecuroides
Pennisetum alopecuroides 'Hameln'

ight yellow *Chasmanthium latifolium* (northern sea oats)

autumn colour

bronze

The North American native *Schizachyrium scoparium* (little bluestem) in Niagara Park's Botanical Gardens. A fiery red in autumn it grows naturally on hillsides and meadows and can be used in the flower border or for naturalizing. It grows about 2 feet (60 cm) high and wide. Tiny, translucent flowers are produced along the upper two-thirds of its stems in late September. It needs good drainage with a lot of sun. It has a tendency to self-seed.

more autumn bronzes
Miscanthus sinensis 'Huron Sentinel'
Miscanthus sinensis 'Graziella'
Saccharum ravennae (formerly *Erianthus ravennae*)

bronze *Schizachyrium scoparium* (little bluestem)

winter colour

blonde

Miscanthus sinensis 'Gracillimus'
Miscanthus sinensis 'Silberfeder'
Miscanthus sinensis 'Grosse Fontäne'
Miscanthus sinensis 'Malepartus'
Panicum virgatum 'Heavy Metal'
Panicum virgatum 'Warrior'
Pennisetum alopecuroides 'Hameln'

bronze

Carex 'Buchananii'
Hakonechloa macra
Pennisetum alopecuroides and
Chasmanthium latifolium
Schizachyrium scoparium

blue

Helictotrichon sempervirens

special conditions

Many visual artists have celebrated gardens with paints, textiles and glass. Poets, essayists and novelists have placed the ideal garden as a central metaphor in their works. But most of us work in ordinary patches where growing conditions are not ideal. And most of us cherish the magic of serendipity, bungling coincidence and dreams — realized or not — that personalize our garden spaces.

The following pages address a universe that includes deserts, scrublands and rock, patches of land beside sun-stealing high-rise buildings, dense woodland, bush, shaded valleys and long, cold winters.

winter

Before we introduced ornamental grasses, our winter garden was a naked shadow of its charmed summer self.

Miscanthus sinensis 'Huron Sunrise' in summer

We delighted in the lacy branches of the old oaks and maples against the sky and depended on the birch trees in the front garden for their bright bark. The spruce gave us a bit of blue; glossy wide-leafed hostas and mock holly added some green, other evergreen shapes and shades threw in some variation. But ornamental grasses have trans-formed our winter landscape.

The foliage, plumes and tassels capture the sun magnificently on a sparkling white background. Freezing rain turns every leaf and stem into a glass wonderland. Silhouetted against the low winter light, grasses are almost free of colour, creating a monochromatic moving picture amid the ruins of summer annuals and perennials.

Whether upright divergent, mounded or arching, ornamental grass archi-tecture is most apparent and splendid in winter.

There is no better group of plants to highlight seasonal glories than grasses. *Miscanthus sinensis* 'Huron Sunrise' in summer and winter.

Miscanthus sinensis 'Huron Sunrise' in winter

Carex buchananii

Carex buchananii pokes through the first snow like a four-dimensional line drawing. This petite tufted sedge with thin round leaves and curled tips is 2 feet (60 cm) high and 14 inches (36 cm) wide.

Hakonechloa macra is one of the most elegant of groundcovers. Its bamboo-like 1-foot (30-cm) arching leaves grow in 2-feet (60-cm) mounds.

Hakonechloa macra

winter

Helictotrichon sempervirens (blue oat grass)

A group of 10 *Helictotrichon sempervirens* (blue oat grass) accent the junction of two pathways in an Exeter, Ontario, planting. The metallic blue leaves of summer, now a jubilant winter yellow, give texture to the snowy landscape.

With a tall Clumner spruce, the finely structured *Miscanthus sinensis* 'Gracillimus' provides a flourish of blonde contrast and seasonal flamboyance.

Miscanthus sinensis 'Gracillimus'

Miscanthus sinensis 'Silberfeder'

Miscanthus sinensis 'Silberfeder' is more upright in structure and has wider leaves than 'Gracillimus.' Its winter halo of downy white plumes are superb snow catchers.

A 6-foot (1.8-m) snow-bound *Miscanthus sinensis* 'Malepartus' arches under the weight of snow. This robust, upright plant with a 5-foot (1.5-m) girth turns silver blonde in winter.

Miscanthus sinensis 'Malepartus'

winter

Panicum virgatum 'Warrior'

The open, arching structure of *Panicum virgatum* 'Warrior' brings animation to winter settings. It grows to 4 feet (1.2 m) across.

Pennisetum alopecuroides with *Chasmanthium latifolium* in the background. The structural delicacy of this medium-sized grass transforms to a crystal fountain in snow and frost.

Pennisetum alopecuroides
(*Chasmanthium latifolium* in background)

ennisetum alopecuroides 'Hameln'

An elegant *Pennisetum alopecuroides* 'Hameln' arches in front of a snow-covered rock installation.

Medium-sized *Schizachyrium scoparium* (little bluestem) is a great naturalizing plant that gives contrasting texture and colour to this planting of juniper.

chizachyrium scoparium (little bluestem)

wetlands

Wetlands occur in low-lying areas near freshwater lakes, ponds, streams and rivers, or near salt water in coastal areas.

Miscanthus floridulus in wet conditions

In wetlands, the water is usually at, above, or just below the land surface. Only plants that don't mind having wet feet thrive under these conditions.

Besides providing important wildlife habitat, wetlands help prevent flooding and clean contaminated water through natural filtering processes. All of the ornamental grasses in this section thrive in damp, moist conditions near ponds and streams. Some even do well in extreme conditions, like bogs and marshes. Most of the plants here will grow in drier soil too, but they behave differently without moisture. In dry conditions, *Miscanthus floridulus*, for example, will grow only 5 feet (1.5 m) high with a few green leaves among a number of dry-looking brown leaves. With plenty of moisture it can grow from 12 to 14 feet (3.7 to 4.4 m) high with an abundance of rich green leaves well into autumn.

Miscanthus floridulus in dry conditions

rundo donax

Arundo donax is a heavy drinker. The wetter and hotter it is the better it grows. It grows up to 14 feet (3.6 m) and can get much taller in a hot, wet season. Here it is pictured with *Pennisetum setaceum* 'Rubrum' at Waterloo Gardens in Philadelphia.

Miscanthus sinensis 'Huron Sunrise' and *Miscanthus sinensis* 'Variegatus' side by side in moist, heavy clay soil. Most *Miscanthus* species, particularly the larger-leafed ones, do well in both moist and dry conditions. Try planting these in a moist spot with the magnificent *Ligularia* 'The Rocket.'

Miscanthus sinensis 'Huron Sunrise' and
Miscanthus sinensis 'Variegatus'

wetlands

Miscanthus sinensis 'Strictus' (porcupine grass) at Niagara Parks Botanical Gardens, Niagara Falls, Ontario. With its yellow horizontal striping, height of 5 feet (1.5 m) and width of 4 feet (1.2 m), 'Strictus' makes a great specimen plant. It creates magic when planted near long-flowering *Gaura lindheimeri* 'Whirling Butterflies' or 'Siskiyou Pink.'

Miscanthus sinensis 'Strictus' (porcupine grass)

A young *Molinia caerulea* ssp. arundinacea
'Skyracer' is already about 6 feet (1.8 m)
tall in Kurt Bluemel's garden near
Baltimore. *Molinia* species will grow in
either moist or dry conditions. Planted
with *Rodgersia pinnata* 'Superba,' with
its larger leaf structure and pink flower
spikes, the texture and colour of
'Skyracer' are electric.

Molinia caerulea ssp. **arundinacea** 'Skyracer'

wetlands

Panicum virgatum 'Warrior'

Panicum virgatum 'Warrior' has a purple leaf and a lovely metallic flower that also turns purple in the autumn. It has an upright divergent habit and grows in moist conditions. 'Warrior' grows about 3 feet (90 cm) high and about 4 feet (1.2 m) wide. A good companion plant is *Kirengeshoma palmate* (waxbells), which has maple-like leaves and drooping yellow flowers in late summer.

Phalaris arundinacea 'Feesey's Form' provides good erosion control and makes a great container plant. We planted 300 one-gallon pots to stop water from washing out the eighteenth green at Islington Golf and Country Club in Toronto. 'Feesey's Form' is invasive and must be spaded each spring for control. It has a variegated white and green leaf with a line of pink in the white area. It grows from 2 to 3 feet (60 to 90 cm) tall and can spread to 5 feet (1.5 m) or more if not controlled.

Phalaris arundinacea 'Feesey's Form'

Alopecurus pratensis 'Aureus'

Alopecurus pratensis 'Aureus' has a yellow and green variegation and performs well in moist conditions, near ponds or streams.

A young stand of *Arundo donax* 'Variegata' at 6 to 9 feet (1.8 to 2.7 m) tall and 2 to 3 feet (60 to 90 cm) wide. This grass can grow up to 5 feet (1.5 m) wide. It has a stunning green leaf with a wide white stripe. It illuminates the whole area and is an instant eye-catcher in the garden.

Arundo donax 'Variegata'

dry conditions

Analyzing a garden's microclimate is an essential part of picking the most appropriate grass.

Miscanthus sinensis 'Puenktchen' tolerates dry and moist conditions

Six or seven centuries ago, repeated droughts forced First Nations peoples to abandon entire areas of the Southwest in North America. In the last century, a tragic drought in the 1930s turned vast areas of the Prairies and Great Plains into dust bowls. Major droughts still occur roughly every 22 years in North America.

A drought is not the same as a dry climate. Drought is a condition that is temporary, although it may last for years. Most gardeners have to contend with partial droughts, or dry spells, brought on by 14 or more days without enough rain.

Ornamental grass gardeners in dry climates can choose from a good selection of plants. In more temperate climates many grasses easily weather dry spells that can devastate other perennials and annuals.

Helictotrichon sempervirens (blue oat grass) tolerates drought conditions

tolerates dry and moist conditions

Calamagrostis, Panicum and *Pennisetum* species grow well in both dry and moist conditions.

tolerates drought conditions

Helictotrichon sempervirens (blue oat grass) does well in drought as do many of the fine-leafed varieties of *Miscanthus sinensis,* such as 'Gracillimus,' 'Berlin,' 'Morning Light,' and 'Puenktchen.'

Most of the *Festuca* species, including the very popular 'Elijah Blue' and 'Superba,' tolerate drought well.

dry conditions

Miscanthus sinensis 'Berlin'

Miscanthus sinensis 'Berlin' tolerates very dry conditions. This newer selection has a spectacular golden flower and can grow to 6 feet (1.8 m). There are five plants in this installation.

Bouteloua curtipendula (mosquito grass), a native grass, has a wonderful open structure. In flower it looks like a little cloud of mosquitoes, hence the common name.

Bouteloua curtipendula (mosquito grass)

Pennisetum messiacum 'Red Bunny Tails'

Pennisetum messiacum 'Red Bunny Tails' tolerates dry conditions and flowers in pretty red plumes.

A grouping of *Helictotrichon sempervirens* (blue oat grass).

Helictotrichon sempervirens (blue oat grass)

dry conditions

Variegated **Miscanthus sinensis** 'Puenktchen'

Variegated *Miscanthus sinensis* 'Puenktchen' tolerates dry conditions well.

The fine-leafed *Miscanthus sinensis* 'Morning Light' grows to approximately 4 feet (1.2 m) high and about 3 feet (90 cm) in overall width.

Miscanthus sinensis 'Morning Light'

orghastrum nutans

The magnificent, metallic blue native grass, *Sorghastrum nutans,* growing beside *Rudbeckia* 'Goldsturm.'

Deschampsia cespitosa by a water fountain in the Van Dusen Gardens in British Columbia.

eschampsia cespitosa

shade

Many gardeners, particularly in urban areas, face challenges of gardening in the shade. I am asked more questions about shade-tolerant plants than almost anything else.

People who think of grasses as only sun-loving are pleased to learn that many do not require a sunny site. Grass-like *Carex* species especially do well in shade.

Calamagrostis arundinacea var. *brachytricha* in autumn. It flowers late in early September on upright divergent foliage that grows to 30 inches (75 cm) tall and about 2 feet (60 cm) wide. It makes a wonderful cut flower.

Calamagrostis arundinacea var. **brachytricha**

arex conica 'Variegata'

Carex conica 'Variegata' is the smallest *Carex* we grow. It reaches only 4 to 6 inches (10 to 15 cm) in height and about 6 to 8 inches (15 to 20 cm) in width. The fine-textured blue-green leaves have a white stripe. It works well as a specimen plant in rock gardens or as a ground cover at the feet of *Viburnum lantana*.

Carex albula 'Frosty Curls.' A small, fine, mounded plant, it likes moist shade and grows well in containers. The lime green colour harmonizes with and intensifies companion plants like *Heuchera* 'Pewter Veil' (coral bells) with its burgundy and silver leaves.

arex albula 'Frosty Curls'

shade

Carex japonica

A vigorous, year-old, emerald green *Carex japonica*. In one season it has grown from 6 inches (15 cm) wide in a one-gallon pot to 2 feet (60 cm) inches wide and 10 inches (25 cm) in height. It appears to be quite happy with the half-day of sun and half-day of shade it receives under the *Acer platanoides* 'Crimson King' (red maple) in our front garden. Try planting *C. japonica* with *Persicaria* 'Variegata.'

A young *Carex morrowii* 'Ice Dance.' It's about the same shape and size as its close relative 'Evergold' but 'Ice Dance' has a much thicker leaf and the opposite leaf colour, a white edge on green. It works well as a groundcover with medium-sized *Tiara Hostas*.

Carex morrowii 'Ice Dance'

arex oshimensis 'Evergold'

Carex oshimensis 'Evergold' in a shady
rock garden near Chesley, Ontario.
The small mound in the middle right,
this grass has a variegated white centre
with green-edged leaf. It grows about
1 foot (30 cm) high with an 18-inch
(45-cm) spread. Here it is planted with
other shade or semi-shade plants,
including *Euonymus* in the upper left.

Molinia caerulea 'Moorhexe' (purple
moor grass). All *Molinia* species grow in
shade. 'Moorhexe' is one of the smallest
cultivars, growing to about 1 foot (30 cm)
in height and 2 feet (60 cm) wide at
maturity. It has green foliage and
golden-bronze flowers. It adds an open,
airy presence to the garden and the
foliage turns a lovely yellow in the
autumn. Plant it in front of *Miscanthus
sinensis*, with *Geranium* 'Ann Folkard' at
its feet, for a lovely layered effect.

Molinia caerulea 'Moorhexe' (purple moor grass)

designing with grasses

Pioneer gardener Gertrude Jekyll had a profound understanding of the art of gardening. In *Colour Schemes for the
Flower Garden*, originally published in 1908, a gently dog-
matic Jekyll sharply differentiated between "a collection
of plants" and "a garden," comparing a collection of
plants to a box of paints in wait of a painter.

The following pages address a universe that includes
deserts, scrublands and rock, patches of land beside sun-

stealing high-rise buildings, dense woodland, bush,
shaded valleys and long cold winters.

Chapter two introduced you to the ornamental grass
paint box — an array of temperaments and colours from
which to select. As with all gardening, it's important to
put the right grass in the right place, taking into consid-
eration specifics like drainage, sunlight and shade, as well
as the characteristics, needs and limitations of the plants

Height, structure, growth habit, texture, colour and seasons of interest are some of the variables.

If plants are the paints in garden composition, then the land — its contours and climate — is the canvas. Creative placement of grasses can impart balance and harmony, provide a stunning focal point or create a sense of unity with large plantings.

The first step in creating a garden is to determine what it will be used for — the intent of the garden. If space is not a problem, it can be divided into quite disparate areas. Perhaps there might be a place for reflection or contemplation, a more open area for children's play and recreation, sheltered areas for dining or special settings for garden sculpture. Other considerations might be interesting pathways for walking, fountains, pools, seating, walls, patios, steps or small structures like trellises. The overall design, or theme, of the garden will determine many of these elements.

There are many schools of thought about garden design, from English cottage to Japanese to Mediterranean. While some approach design from this cultural or historic perspective, others, like us, find the most powerful gardens are those that are designed around the selection of the plants themselves. Whatever the focus, all designs begin by establishing the scale, focal point, perspective and proportion in a planting, using the elementary principles of geometry—line, angle, circle, square and triangle.

Unlike a painting, a garden is a moveable feast of change, which raises the second step in garden design — timing. There is no better group of plants to highlight seasonal glories than grasses. As all-season performers, ornamental grasses adapt to natural land formations in dramatic, bold sweeps. They work equally well delineating space, echoing curves and creating screens and borders. Year round, they make superb companions

for bulbs, conifers, perennials, shrubs and trees.

Grasses can be used to create exciting new displays, such as a mass planting of a single specimen to create a natural panorama, or to refresh existing beds. Weaving grasses through an established flower bed will give it a new life with texture, colour and punctuation. Ornamental grasses are suited to a wide range of gardens — natural or formal, large or small — they are as suited to the close-up views in the small walled garden of a townhouse as they are to spacious parks with open vistas.

Four Design Principles

For simplicity, when we select grasses for a design, we use four organizing principles — specimen, scaffold, decorative and natural. Many grasses are versatile enough to fit into more than one of these categories, depending on the setting and the ingenuity of the gardener. The following photographs illustrate how various grasses are used according to these four design principles.

decorative

natural

specimens

Like the leading lady in a play, a specimen grass has enough character to do a
scene alone in the spotlight. These grasses are focal points.

Specimens are selected for unique
architectural structure, pleasing foliage
or exceptional flower display. They
must have enough character to com-
mand attention in beds, borders or
containers, but they are not necessarily
tall. Many medium- and even small-
sized grasses perform well in this role.

Miscanthus sinensis 'Huron Sunrise' is a
fine focal point. It grows to a height of
about 4 feet (1.2 m) and flowers early
with a rich burgundy flower. It is a
wonderful overall performer in dry or
moist conditions.

Miscanthus sinensis 'Huron Sunrise'

ennisetum setaceum 'Burgundy Giant'

This tender *Pennisetum setaceum* 'Burgundy Giant' (giant purple fountain grass) at Longwood Gardens in Maryland is not hardy in Ontario, where we treat it as an annual. It can grow to about 5 feet (1.5 metres).

Arundo donax 'Variegata' (giant variegated reed grass) has white variegated foliage. It is pictured here behind some *Pennisetum alopecuroides* 'Hameln' and a distinctive garden sculpture in Waterloo Gardens, Philadelphia. 'Variegata' thrives in dry or wet conditions and can tower to more than 9 feet (2.7 m) with a girth of 5 feet (1.5 m) in one season.

rundo donax 'Variegata' (giant variegated reed grass)

specimens

A three-year-old *Miscanthus sinensis* 'Cabaret' (Japanese silver grass) at the Walters Gardens in Zeeland, Michigan. Its 1-inch-wide (2.5-cm) leaves have a cream-white midrib and narrow, dark green margins. It is the boldest of the variegated *M. sinensis* cultivars at a height of about 5 feet (1.5 m) and width of 5 feet (1.5 m). Coupled with fabulous variegated foliage it is a fine focal point.

Miscanthus sinensis 'Cabaret' (Japanese silver grass)

ennisetum alopecuroides 'Little Bunny'

One of the miniature contenders in the specimen category is *Pennisetum alopecuroides* 'Little Bunny.' This hardy little member of the fountain grass family has delightful light green foliage and a pale yellow flower in fall. It grows in small clumps and at maturity will be about 8 inches (20 cm) high and 18 inches (45 cm) wide. 'Little Bunny' likes moisture and looks great in a rock garden or near a pond or stream. It is more hardy than its variegated sister 'Little Honey.'

Calamagrostis x *acutiflora* 'Karl Foerster,' shown here in a mass planting, also stands alone magnificently. It grows to about 30 inches (75 cm) high and wide and flowers very early. It is spectacular with the blue-flowering *Perovskia atriplicifolia* and *Saccharum ravennae* (hardy pampas grass).

alamagrostis x **acutiflora** 'Karl Foerster'

scaffolds

Scaffold grasses are the chorus that backs up a diva — the framework that supports and integrates a garden plan.

They form the grid for the garden as a whole and for individual beds. Think of traditional boxwood hedges, which divide a garden into areas for privacy, shelter or atmosphere; in high season they are always eclipsed by showier shrubs and perennials.

When designing with grasses, it is especially important to know what they look like in fall and winter when they are most visible. We favour the hardiest selections with strong outlines that maintain their shape whatever the weather. We select plants with distinctive flower heads that will stay neat or keep their shape throughout the winter. In the top spots in this category are *Miscanthus sinensis* 'Zebrinus,' *Molinia caerulea* ssp. *arundinacea* 'Skyracer' and *Miscanthus sinensis* 'Malepartus.'

Miscanthus sinensis 'Malepartus'

Molinia caerulea ssp. **arundinacea** 'Skyracer'

Molinia caerulea ssp. *arundinacea* 'Skyracer' is the largest plant in this bed of mixed grasses at St. Andrew's Golf Course in Toronto, Ontario.

Striped *Miscanthus sinensis* 'Zebrinus' anchors this front yard mixed perennial bed in Strathroy, Ontario.

Miscanthus sinensis 'Zebrinus'

decoratives

The function of grasses in the decorative category is to provide infill or accent for focal points — a supporting, rather than a starring, role. Decoratives dramatize a planting with sound, light and motion.

Calamagrostis x **acutiflora** 'Karl Foerster'

Calamagrostis x *acutiflora* 'Karl Foerster' poolside in Bala, Ontario. It grows 30 inches (75 cm) high and wide and has a bronze flower in mid- to late summer. It works very well with *Coreopsis* 'Moonbeam' and *Miscanthus sinensis* 'Malepartus.'

The illuminating *Miscanthus sinensis* 'Variegatus' was one of the first grasses we put into a garden setting. A fine specimen plant, it grows to 6 feet (1.8 m) and is pictured here in our production field. Although it is showing a brown flower, 'Variegatus' rarely flowers in Ontario and only where the summers are hottest.

Miscanthus sinensis 'Variegatus'

anicum virgatum 'Heavy Metal'

Panicum virgatum 'Heavy Metal' has a stunning metallic blue colour that changes to purple in the fall. Unlike some of its relatives, 'Heavy Metal' is very tight and erect in structure. It can grow to a height of about 3 feet (90 cm).

Chasmanthium latifolium is noted for both foliage and flower. It is used for erosion control and also in the garden. Its colour progresses from green in summer to copper in autumn, when oat-like flowers bow gracefully from the arching stems.

hasmanthium latifolium

decoratives

Panicum virgatum 'Huron Solstice'

The outstanding copper-leafed *Panicum virgatum* 'Huron Solstice' is a recent introduction. Erect in structure, it grows to 3 feet (90 cm) high and wide.

Molinia caerulea 'Variegata' (striped purple moor grass) has cream and green leaves. Depending on the moisture it grows to a height of only 2 to 3 feet (60 to 90 cm). 'Variegata' is slow to mature but it produces superb wheat-coloured flowers on yellow stems that turn purple with pollen as the season moves on. Here it is planted with sweet-scented lavender. In the foreground is a fragrant *Buddleia davidii* (butterfly bush).

Molinia caerulea 'Variegata' (striped purple moor grass)

ennisetum alopecuroides 'Moudry' (black-flowering pennisetum)

This *Pennisetum alopecuroides* 'Moudry' (black-flowering pennisetum) is about three years old, 30 inches (70 cm) across and 2 feet (60 cm) high. Its spectacular flowers don't appear in the first year or two and don't elongate like 'Rubrum.' A mature plant produces distinctive cascading flowers of deep purple that are radiant in the autumn light.

The best-selling perennial grass for years has been *Helictotrichon sempervirens* (blue oat grass). It is very compact and maintains its striking metallic blue colour into late fall. This versatile plant grows to about 18 inches (45 cm) across and 2 feet (60 cm) tall and tolerates extreme conditions, from dry to wet and sun to shade. Its fine texture complements many different plants. We like to contrast it with the textures of *Artemisia arborescens* 'Powis Castle' and *Heuchera* 'Chocolate Ruffles.'

Helictotrichon sempervirens (blue oat grass)

naturals

The first European settlers in North America described the tall grass prairie as a
sea of amber waves. Native grasses — or naturals — are not visitors.

Rooted in North American climate
zones, they propagate easily and are
extremely hardy, unlike some imported
grasses. Native grasses are used in
prairie restoration work, for naturalizing
and for erosion control. They also have
a role to play in garden design.

Native to wet prairies and marshes from Maine
to the great plains of North America, the tall
variegated *Spartina pectinata* 'Aureomarginata'
(prairie cord grass)

Spartina pectinata 'Aureomarginata' (prairie cord grass)

tallest

Saccharum ravennae in flower towers to 15 feet (4.6 m). This is a cousin of the majestic native grass *Saccharum giganteum*.

tall

Andropogon gerardii (big bluestem) is sturdy, upright and clump-forming. It can grow to over 6 feet (2 m).

Sorghastrum nutans (Indian grass) is one of the most abundant and beautiful tall grasses in the original prairies. It is non-invasive and ideal for naturalizing. Its wonderful bronze flower and metallic blue foliage make it a favourite native grass for the garden as well.

medium

Chasmanthium latifolium (northern sea oats), a deep-rooted grass that can tolerate extremely dry conditions, is being widely used in gardens as well as for erosion control on the eastern seaboard. With a foliage height of 3 to 4 feet (.9 to 1.2 m) and a flower height of 5 to 6 six feet (1.5 to 1.8 m).

Leymus arenarius glauca (blue lyme grass), usually found around the edges of lakes and streams in dry, sandy conditions, is very effective for erosion control. Although the flower seeds are edible, it is an invasive spreader. Unless it is in a container, we don't recommend using it in the garden.

naturals

Andropogon gerardii (big bluestem)

Andropogon gerardii (big bluestem) with a contrasting hardy bamboo. The stems of *A. gerardii* turn blue as summer ends.

Bouteloua curtipendula

In fall, the showy foliage of *Bouteloua curtipendula* turns yellow and its spectacular 2 feet (60-cm) spikelets rise well above the foot-high (30-cm) basal foliage to wave like ribbons in the wind. Remarkably, the flowers temporarily blush back to their summer purple with the first frost.

This variegated *Deschampsia cespitosa* 'Northern Lights' does not like full sun. It grows best in moist conditions and dappled shade.

Deschampsia cespitosa 'Northern Lights'. 'Northern Lights' was developed from the native grass *Deschampsia cespitosa*.

naturals

Saccharum ravennae (hardy pampas grass), in flower a magnificent 15-foot (4.6-m) giant, performs well as a single specimen, a decorative or in mass plantings.

Saccharum ravennae

Hordeum jubatum

Almost every *Hordeum jubatum* (foxtail barley) seed that matures is viable. It is fine in the garden if cut back before seeds mature. It is good for naturalizing and birds love it. *H. jubatum* grows about 18 inches (45 cm) high and about 2 feet (60 cm) wide. Flowers have a purple pink hue and look wonderful as a cut flower before the seeds mature.

Hystrix patula (bottlebrush grass) is named for its flower shape. It grows about 1 to 3 feet (30 to 90 cm) high and about the same in overall width. It is a good border plant for use in natural woodland settings.

Hystrix patula (bottlebrush grass)

naturals

Sorghastrum nutans 'Sioux Blue,' a North American native known for its yellow tone in the autumn, is used for naturalizing. It grows in very dry conditions and in all kinds of soil from sandy to heavy clay.

Sorghastrum nutans 'Sioux Blue'

Panicum virgatum

The open panicles and stunning yellow autumn colour of *Panicum virgatum* make it a great addition to a mixed border garden. *P. virgatum* is native to Ontario.

Medium-sized *Sporobolus heterolepis* (prairie dropseed) wears lovely bronze tones in autumn.

Sporobolus heterolepis

layering

Layering is one of the most exciting challenges when designing with ornamental grasses. It requires planning with an understanding of the plants' growth habits, structures and needs, but most of all, it takes time and experimentation. A good starting point is to consider the size of grasses. The lists below suggests several grasses in the tall, medium and small categories.

By paying close attention to the particulars of shape, leaf structure, flowers, growth habit and seasonal colour within each size category, you will be on your way to becoming a practitioner of the art of layering with ornamental grasses.

layering

Miscanthus sinensis 'Huron Blush'

The foliage of the miniature *Miscanthus sinensis* 'Huron Blush' is only about 2 feet (60 cm) high, but when it is in flower the stems and delicate pink panicles tower through and above the foliage to 4 feet (1.2 m). *M. sinensis* 'Grosse Fontäne,' grows to 8 feet (2.4 m) and has a similar flower stretch, but 'Huron Blush' is the only small variety of this species with such a magnificent characteristic. The wide leaves of 'Huron Blush' distinguish it from most other *M. sinensis* cultivars, which are generally very fine-leafed.

Small grasses
(to 1 foot/ 30 cm)

Arrhenatherum elatius ssp. *bulbosum*
'Variegatus' (bulbous oat grass)

Carex albula 'Frosty Curls'
(Frosty Curls hair sedge)

Carex bergrenii

Carex comans (New Zealand hair sedge)

Carex conica 'Variegata'
(miniature variegated sedge)

Carex morrowii 'Ice Dance' (Ice Dance sedge)

Carex morrowii aureo variegata
(silver variegated Japanese sedge)

Festuca glauca 'Boulder Blue' (blue fescue)

Hakonechloa macra (hakone grass)

Holcus mollis 'Albo-variegatus'
(variegated velvet grass)

Imperata cylindrica 'Red Baron'
(Japanese blood grass)

Koeleria glauca (large blue hair grass)

layering

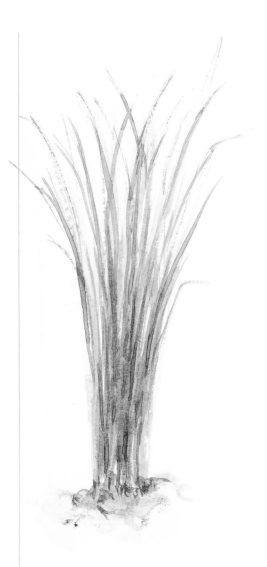

medium grasses

medium grasses
(1 to 5 feet / 30 cm to 1.5 m)

Bouteloua curtipendula (side oats gramma)

Calamagrostis arundinacea var. *brachytricha*
(fall-blooming reed grass)

Calamagrostis x acutiflora (Karl Foerster)

Calamagrostis (Overdam)

Carex buchananii (leather leaf sedge)

Carex elata 'Bowles' Golden' (yellow sedge)

Carex muskingumensis (palm sedge)

Carex japonica (Japanese sedge)

Chasmanthium latifolium (northern sea oats)

Deschampsia cespitosa (tufted hair grass)

Festuca amethystina (blue fescue)

Helictotrichon sempervirens (blue oat grass)

Hordeum jubatum (foxtail barley)

Hystrix patula (bottlebrush grass)

Leymus arenarius 'Glaucus' (giant dune grass)

Molinia caerulea (moor grass)

Molinia caerulea 'Variegata' (variegated moor
grass)

Panicum virgatum (switch grass)

Pennisetum alopecuroides (hardy fountain grass)

Pennisetum alopecuroides 'Hameln'
(miniature fountain grass)

medium grasses (continued)

Phalaris arundinacea (ribbon grass)

Schizachyrium scoparium (little bluestem)

Sporobolus heterolepis (prairie dropseed)

tall grasses
(6 feet / 1.8 m and over)

Arundo donax (giant reed)

Spartina pectinata (prairie cord grass)

Andropogon gerardii (big bluestem)

Molinia caerulea ssp. *arundinacea* 'Skyracer'
(purple moor grass)

Miscanthus sinensis (maiden grass)

Saccharum ravennae (hardy pampas grass)

Sorghastrum nutans 'Sioux Blue' (Indian grass)

tall grasses

simple garden plans

These garden plans are meant to encourage you to create your own grass garden
or to mix and match your favourite shrubs and perennials with grasses. Recreate
the plans in your garden or use them as a starting point for your own ideas.

For the most dramatic entry into grass gardening try planting a group with just one variety. Below is a simple group planting of *Panicum virgatum* 'Heavy Metal' around a bench structure at Longwood Gardens in Pennsylvania.

anicum virgatum 'Heavy Metal'

simple garden plans

This simple and attractive bed contrasts two colourful grasses with a grouping of four upright conifers.

grasses with upright conifers

A *Juniperus communis 'Witchita'*

B *Imperata cylindrica 'Red Baron'*

C *Festuca glauca 'Elijah Blue'*

mperata cylindrica 'Red Baron'

simple garden plans

This more complex design features a grouping of four spectacular specimens
surrounded by a scaffold of 16 grasses and decorated with 14 *Pennisetum
alopecuroides* 'Hameln,' and 50 *Helictotrichon sempervirens.*

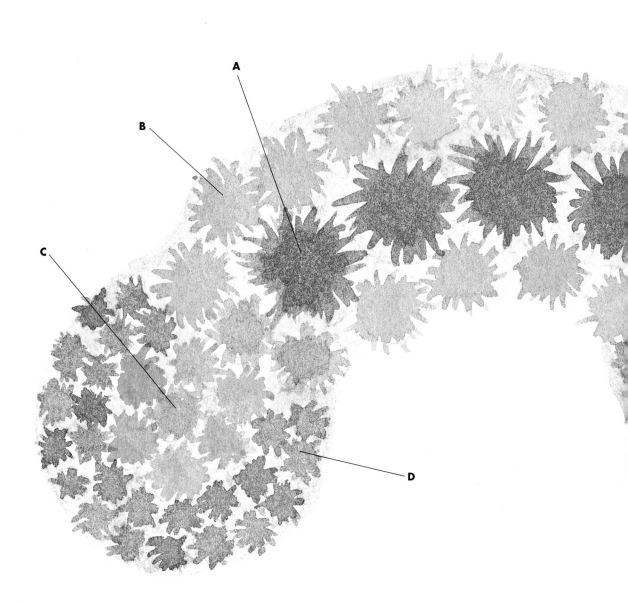

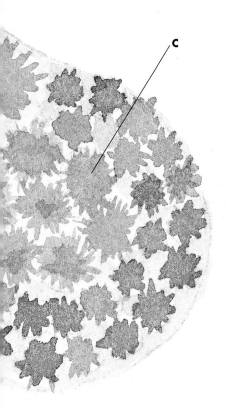

A *Molinia caerulea* ssp. *arundinacea* 'Skyracer' (4)

B *Panicum virgatum* 'Warrior'(16)

C *Pennisetum alopecuroides* 'Hameln' (14)

D *Helictotrichon sempervirens* (50)

simple garden plans

My sister Nancy Potter transformed her front yard when she installed four
grasses in an existing perennial bed.

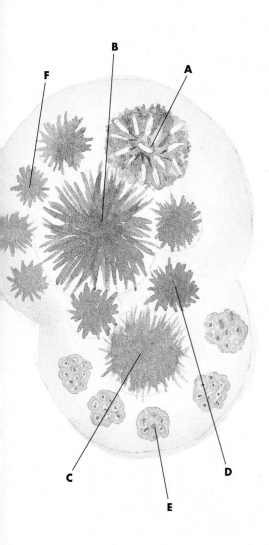

A *Buddleia* 'White Profusion'

B *Miscanthus sinensis* 'Malepartus'

C *Calamagrostis x acutiflora* 'Overdam'

D *Helictotrichon sempervirens*

E *Coreopsis* 'Moonbeam'

F *Pennisetum alopecuroides* 'Hameln'

simple garden plans

There are eight grasses in this adventuresome, kidney-shaped corner bed designed by enthusiast Jim Dalton in 2002, suggesting how many perennials and shrubs grow well with grasses. Like most avid gardeners, Jim is already making changes.

A *Prunus 'Newport'*

B *Cornus alba 'Sibirica Variegata'*

C *Helictotrichon sempervirens*

D *Geraniun cantabrigiense 'Biokova'*

E *Calamagrostis x acutiflora 'Karl Foerster'*

F *Molinia caerulea* ssp. *arundinacea* 'Skyracer'

G *Miscanthus sinensis 'Graziella'*

H *Deschampsia cespitosa*

I *Arundo donax*

J *Sedum 'Autumn Joy'*

K *Festuca ovina glauca*

L *Pennisetum alopecuroides 'Hameln'*

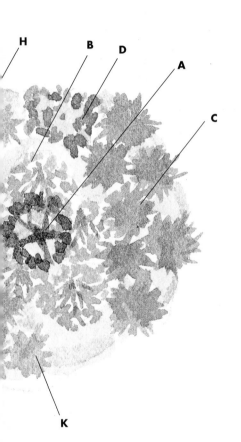

simple garden plans

Calamagrostis x *acutiflora* 'Karl Foerster' in a group planting at a Canada/USA border crossing, with water, stone and a bronze sculpture.

Calamagrostis x **acutiflora** 'Karl Foerster'

iscanthus sinensis and **Pennisetum alopecuroides**

Miscanthus sinensis and *Pennisetum alopecuroides* in a mixed border at the Royal Botanical Gardens in Hamilton, Ontario.

A partly shaded garden with *Calamagrostis arundinacea* var. *brachytricha* and hosta in Bala, Ontario.

alamagrostis arundinacea var. **brachytricha**

simple garden plans

Miscanthus sinensis 'Gracillimus' and *Pennisetum alopecuroides* accenting a garden bench in a small townhouse.

Miscanthus sinensis 'Gracillimus' and
Pennisetum alopecuroides

estuca glauca

Festuca glauca mass planting on a hill at Westridge Farms in Langley, BC.

Pennisetum alopecuroides 'Hameln' and the golden hues of *Stipa gigantea* at Kurt Bluemel's pond garden near Baltimore, Maryland.

ennisetum alopecuroides 'Hameln' in foreground

simple garden plans

Miscanthus sinensis 'Variegatus' and **Miscanthus sinensis** 'Strictus'

Miscanthus sinensis 'Variegatus' and *Miscanthus sinensis* 'Strictus' in autumn at the Cuddy garden in Strathroy, Ontario.

Miscanthus sinensis 'Gracillimus' with evergreens and stone landscaping at an office building in Burlington, Ontario.

Miscanthus sinensis 'Gracillimus'

A pink-flowered *Cortaderia selloana* in a Vancouver Island garden.

Cortaderia selloana (pink)

simple garden plans

Miscanthus sinensis 'Huron Sunset' in full burgundy flower.

Miscanthus sinensis 'Huron Sunset'

Pennisetum glaucum (red-leafed millet) a new annual that has great colour and attracts birds.

Pennisetum glaucum (red-leafed millet)

simple garden plans

Miscanthus sinensis 'Huron Penetangore'

Miscanthus sinensis 'Huron Penetangore' (big dot) is a new introduction with only one or two yellow bands on each leaf.

Miscanthus sinensis 'Huron Sunrise,' our first introduction, flowers early with a burgundy flower.

Miscanthus sinensis 'Huron Sunrise'

perennial companions

There are hundreds of perennials that are perfect grass companions — in the sun or shade garden and in all growing and soil conditions. Hostas, ferns and bamboo, however, are especially lovely with hardy ornamental grasses. Evergreen bamboo offers a delightful contrast of colours and textures in the monochromatic winter grass garden. In shade gardens, easy-maintenance ferns and hostas come in a wide range of sizes, shapes, textures and colours.

The following list of favourite grass companions includes botanical and common names, zone hardiness, form, height, flower colour, flowering period and optimal growing conditions. The heights and bloom times are based on Ontario growing conditions.

perennial companions

	Achillea 'Moonshine' (fern-leafed yarrow)	**Artemisia arborescens 'Powis Castle'** (wormwood)
Zone	3–8	4–9
Form and height	Upright; 20" (50 cm)	Upright; 28" (77 cm)
Flower	Yellow	Silver to yellow or soft green
Bloomtime	August to September	Not grown for its flower
Growing conditions	Full sun; drought tolerant	Full sun; drought tolerant

	Anemone 'Honorine Jobert' (windflower)	**Bambusa 'Fargesia'** (bamboo)
Zone	4–9	5–9
Form and height	Upright; 42" (1.5 m)	Upright; 8' (2.5 m)
Flower	White	—
Bloomtime	August to September	Rarely flowers
Growing conditions	Part shade; shade	Full sun to part shade

	Angelica gigas (Angelica)	**Baptisia australis** (wild indigo)
Zone	4	2–9
Form and height	Upright; 42–54" (1.05–1.4 m)	Upright; 3' (90 cm)
Flower	White	Blue
Bloomtime	August to September	June to July
Growing conditions	Full sun	Full sun to part shade; drought tolerant

	Campanula lactiflora (bellflower)	**Crambe cordifolia** (sea kale)
Zone	3–7	5–9
Form and height	Upright; 28" (75 cm)	Upright; 5' (1.5 m)
Flower	Blue	White
Bloomtime	June to July	April to May
Growing conditions	Full sun to part shade	Full sun

	Cimicifuga racemosa 'Cordifolia' (bugbane)	**Echinacea 'Magnus'** (purple cone flower)
Zone	3–9	4–8
Form and height	Upright; 47" (1.2 m)	Upright; 48" (1.2 m)
Flower	White, pink	Purple/red
Bloomtime	August to September	August to September
Growing conditions	Part shade; shade; moisture tolerant	Full sun; drought tolerant

	Coreopsis lanceolata 'Sterntaler' (tickseed)	**Echinops ritro** (globe thistle)
Zone	4–9	2–9
Form and height	Upright; 2' (60 cm)	Upright; 3' (90 cm)
Flower	Yellow	Blue
Bloomtime	June to September	August to September
Growing conditions	Full sun	Full sun

Eupatorium purpureum
(joe pye weed)

Zone	5–9
Form and height	Upright; 70" (1.78 m)
Flower	Pink, white, wine
Bloomtime	August to September
Growing conditions	Full sun to part shade

Euphorbia griffithii 'Fireglow'
(spurge)

Zone	2–9
Form and height	Upright; 28" (71 cm)
Flower	Orange/red
Bloomtime	April to May
Growing conditions	Full sun

Filipendula rubra 'Venuta Magnifica' (meadowsweet)

Zone	2–9
Form and height	Upright; 5' (1.5 m)
Flower	Pink/red
Bloomtime	August to September
Growing conditions	Full sun to part shade; moisture tolerant

Gaura lindheimeri 'Whirling Butterflies' (butterfly flower)

Zone	5–9
Form and height	Upright arching; 28" (71 cm)
Flower	White
Bloomtime	June to September
Growing conditions	Full sun to part shade; drought tolerant

Geranium phaeum
(cranesbill)

Zone	4–9
Form and height	Upright; 28" (71 cm)
Flower	Dark purple
Bloomtime	June to July
Growing conditions	Full sun to part shade; moisture and drought tolerant

Helianthus angustifolius
(sunflower)

Zone	4–9
Form and height	Upright; 7' (2 m)
Flower	Yellow
Bloomtime	September to October
Growing conditions	Full sun; drought tolerant

Hemerocallis 'Hyperion'
(daylily)

Zone	3–9
Form and height	Upright arching; 28" (71 cm)
Flower	Yellow
Bloomtime	June to September
Growing conditions	Full sun to part shade

Heuchera 'Chocolate Ruffles'
(coral bells)

Zone	2–9
Form and height	Upright; 20" (50 cm)
Flower	White
Bloomtime	June to July
Growing conditions	Full sun to shade

	Hosta 'Blue Angel' (plantain lily)	Matteuccia struthiopteris (ostrich fern)
Zone	2–9	1–9
Form and height	Upright arching; 3' (90 cm)	Upright; 30"– 5' (75 cm –1.5 m)
Flower	White	Foliage — rich green
Bloomtime	June to July	—
Growing conditions	Part shade to shade; moisture tolerant	Full sun to part shade

	Iris pallida 'Albo Variegata' (iris)	Monarda 'Gardenview Scarlet' (bee balm)
Zone	4–9	3–9
Form and height	Upright; 2' (60 cm)	Upright; 28" (75 cm)
Flower	Fragrant violet flowers	Red
Bloomtime	June to July	June to September
Growing conditions	Sun; well drained	Full sun to part shade

	Knautia macedonica (crimson scabiosa)	Nepeta mussinii 'Dropmore' (catmint)
Zone	5–9	2–9
Form and height	Upright arching; 2' (60 cm)	Prostrate; 10" (25 cm)
Flower	Deep red	Blue
Bloomtime	June to October	June to September
Growing conditions	Full sun	Full sun; drought tolerant

	Ligularia przewalskii (senecio)	Ophiopogon planiscapus 'Ebony Knight' (black mondo grass)
Zone	5–9	5–9
Form and height	Upright; 5' (1.5 m)	Prostrate; 10" (25 cm)
Flower	Yellow spike	Pink flowers/black leaves
Bloomtime	August to September	July to August
Growing conditions	Part shade to sun; moist	Full sun to part shade

Penstemon digitalis 'Husker Red' (beardtongue)

Zone	5–7
Form and height	Upright; 28" (75 cm)
Flower	White
Bloomtime	June to July
Growing conditions	Full sun; drought tolerant

Rodgersia aesculifolia (Rodger's flower)

Zone	5–7
Form and height	Upright arching; 38" (90 cm)
Flower	White
Bloomtime	June to July
Growing conditions	Part shade to shade; moisture tolerant

Perovskia atriplicifolia (russian sage)

Zone	5–8
Form and height	Upright arching; 39" (1 m)
Flower	Blue
Bloomtime	August to October
Growing conditions	Full sun; drought tolerant

Rudbeckia fulgida 'Goldsturm' (black-eyed susan)

Zone	3–8
Form and height	Upright; 20" (60 cm)
Flower	Yellow
Bloomtime	August to September
Growing conditions	Full sun; drought tolerant

Persicaria microcephala 'Red Dragon' (fleece flower)

Zone	3–9
Form and height	Upright; 20" (50 cm)
Flower	Pink, white
Bloomtime	June to July
Growing conditions	Full sun to shade; drought tolerant

Salvia 'Mainacht' (meadow sage)

Zone	4–7
Form and height	Upright; 1' (30 cm)
Flower	Purple
Bloomtime	June to July
Growing conditions	Full sun; drought tolerant

Phlox paniculata (summer phlox)

Zone	3–9
Form and height	Upright; 5' (1.5 m)
Flower	White
Bloomtime	July to August
Growing conditions	Full sun to part shade

Scabiosa columbaria 'Butterfly Blue' (pincushion flower)

Zone	3–8
Form and height	Upright arching; 16" (40 cm)
Flower	Blue
Bloomtime	June to September
Growing conditions	Full sun; drought tolerant

Sedum 'Autumn Joy'
(stonecrop)

Zone	2–9
Form and height	Upright; 2' (60 cm)
Flower	Red
Bloomtime	August to September
Growing conditions	Full sun; drought tolerant

Stachys 'Helene von Stein'
(lamb's ear)

Zone	4–8
Form and height	Prostate; 8"–10" (20–25 cm)
Flower	Lavender
Bloomtime	Rarely flowers
Growing conditions	Full sun; drought tolerant

Thalictrum flavum 'Glaucum'
(meadow rue)

Zone	5–9
Form and height	Upright; 5' (1.5 m)
Flower	Yellow
Bloomtime	July to August
Growing conditions	Part shade; moisture tolerant

Verbascum chaixii 'Album'
(mullein)

Zone	4–9
Form and height	Upright; 39" (1 m)
Flower	White
Bloomtime	June to July
Growing conditions	Full sun; drought tolerant

Veronica longifolia 'Blue Spires' (speedwell)

Zone	3–8
Form and height	Upright; 1'–18" (30–45 cm)
Flower	Blue, rose
Bloomtime	June to July
Growing conditions	Full sun; drought tolerant

Veronicastrum virginicum
(culver's root)

Zone	3–9
Form and height	Upright; 5' (1.5 m)
Flower	White, pink
Bloomtime	June to July
Growing conditions	Full sun to part shade

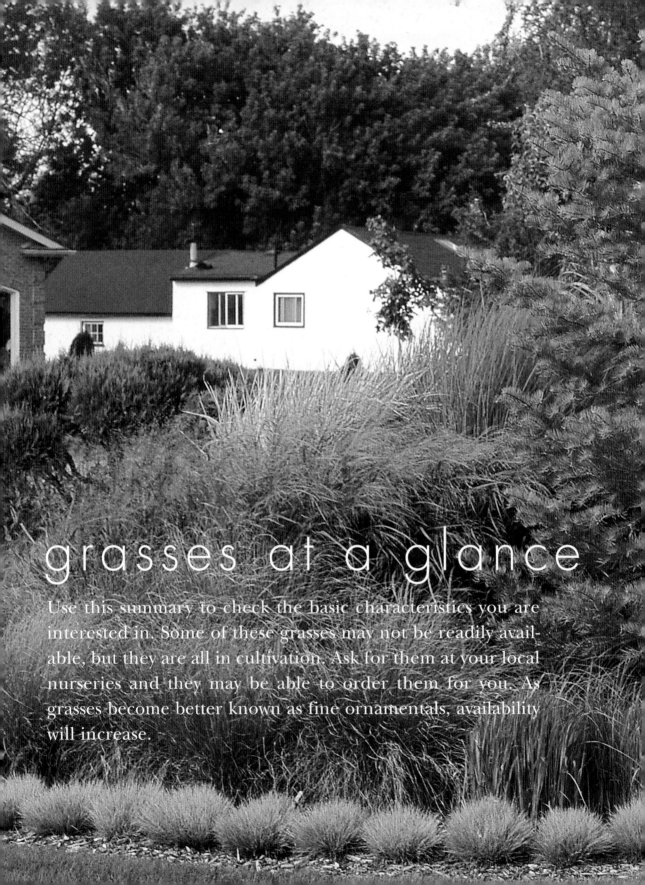

grasses at a glance

Use this summary to check the basic characteristics you are interested in. Some of these grasses may not be readily available, but they are all in cultivation. Ask for them at your local nurseries and they may be able to order them for you. As grasses become better known as fine ornamentals, availability will increase.

Note: In the following listings, where foliage and flowers are very similar, flower height is not mentioned. Where flowers are significantly taller than foliage, the flower height is noted (the flower height is the total height of the plant when in flower). The size is based on average mature growth in average conditions, but these figures can vary based on conditions such as moisture and sun exposure.

grasses at a glance

Acorus gramineus 'Argenteostriatus'
(sweet flag)

Pronunciation	ah-KOR-us gra-MIN-ee-us
Zone	5–9
Form	Small, upright erect
Size	Foliage 10" (25 cm) Width 1' (30 cm)
Finest seasonal colour	Summer white and green variegated
Flower colour & timing	Rarely flowers
Growing conditions	Sun to shade; ordinary garden conditions to moist
Landscape use	Single, mass planting, groundcover
Growth habit	Clumping

Alopecurus pratensis 'Aureus'
(yellow foxtail grass)

Pronunciation	al-o-PEK-u-rus prah-TEN-sis AW-ree-us
Zone	5–9
Form	Medium, tufted
Size	Foliage 6" (15 cm) Flower 18" (45 cm) Width 18" (45 cm)
Finest seasonal colour	Spring to summer yellow and green variegated
Flower colour & timing	Yellowish white, spring
Growing conditions	Sun; ordinary garden conditions to dry
Landscape use	Single, mass planting, groundcover
Growth habit	Clumping

Andropogon gerardii
(big bluestem)

Pronunciation	an-droh-POH-gon jer-AR-dee-eye
Zone	3–9
Form	Tall, upright divergent
Size	Foliage 14" (36 cm) Flower 5' (1.5 m) Width 3' (90 cm)
Finest seasonal colour	Spring bright blue green Autumn copper bronze
Flower colour & timing	Purplish, August–September
Growing conditions	Sun; ordinary garden conditions to dry
Landscape use	Single, naturalizing, specimen
Growth habit	Clumping

Arrhenatherum elatius ssp. **bulbosum 'Variegatus'** (bulbous oat grass)

Pronunciation	ah-ren-AH-ther-um el-AH-tee-us bul-BOH-sum var-ee-uh-GAH-tus
Zone	4–8
Form	Mounded
Size	Foliage 10" (25 cm) Flower 18" (45 cm) Width 1' (30 cm)
Finest seasonal colour	Spring to summer white variegated
Flower colour & timing	Flowers white when produced in early summer
Growing conditions	Partial shade; ordinary garden conditions
Landscape use	Single, containers, mass planting, groundcover
Growth habit	Moderately invasive

grasses at a glance

Pronunciation	**Arundo donax**
	(giant reed)
	ah-RUN-doh DOH-nax
Zone	5–10, much of Zone 4 in milder winters
Form	Tall, upright arching
Size	Foliage 14' (4.3 m) Leaves 3" (7.5 cm) wide
	Flower 15' (4.6 m) Width 6' (1.8 m)
Finest seasonal colour	Spring to summer blue-green
Flower colour & timing	Rarely flowers, except in extremely mild climates
Growing conditions	Sun; ordinary garden conditions to moist
Landscape use	Single, screen, specimen
Growth habit	Moderately invasive

	Arundo donax 'Variegata'
	(striped giant reed)
Pronunciation	ah-RUN-doh DOH-nax var-ee-uh-GAH-tah
Zone	5–10, much of Zone 5 in milder winters
Form	Tall, upright arching
Size	Foliage 9' (2.7 m) Leaves 3" (7.5 cm) wide;
	Flower 10' (3 m) Width 5' (1.5 m)
Finest seasonal colour	Spring to summer white variegated
Flower colour & timing	Rarely flowers
Growing conditions	Sun; ordinary garden conditions to moist
Landscape use	Single, containers, mosaic, specimen
Growth habit	Moderately invasive

Bouteloua curtipendula
(side oats gramma)

Pronunciation	boo-tuh-LOO-ah kur-tih-PEN-dyoo-la
Zone	4–9
Form	Medium, mounded
Size	Foliage 1' (30 cm) Flower 2' (60 cm) Width 2' (60 cm)
Finest seasonal colour	Autumn yellow
Flower colour & timing	Purplish, June
Growing conditions	Sun; ordinary garden conditions to dry
Landscape use	Single, naturalizing, mass planting
Growth habit	Clumping

Briza media
(quaking grass)

Pronunciation	BREYE-zah MEE-dee-ah
Zone	4–10
Form	Small, mounded
Size	Foliage 1' (30 cm) Flower 18" (45 cm) Width 18" (45 cm)
Finest seasonal colour	Spring to summer green
Flower colour & timing	Green iridescent turning golden, spring
Growing conditions	Sun; ordinary garden conditions
Landscape use	Single, mass planting
Growth habit	Clumping

grasses at a glance

Pronunciation	
Zone	
Form	
Size	
Finest seasonal colour	
Flower colour & timing	
Growing conditions	
Landscape use	
Growth habit	

Bromus inermis 'Skinner's Gold'
(smooth brome)

BRO-mus in-ER-mus

3–9

Medium, arching

Foliage 18" (45 cm) **Flower** 2' (60 cm) **Width** 30" (76 cm)

Summer yellow and green variegated

Golden bronze, summer

Sun; ordinary garden conditions

Single, mass planting, container

Invasive

Pronunciation	
Zone	
Form	
Size	
Finest seasonal colour	
Flower colour & timing	
Growing conditions	
Landscape use	
Growth habit	

Calamagrostis arundinacea var. **brachytricha**
(fall-blooming reed grass)

kal-ah-mah-GROS-tis ah-run-din-AH-see-ah BRAK-ee-trik-ah

5–9

Medium, upright divergent

Foliage 20" (51 cm) **Flower** 3' (90 cm) **Width** 30" (76 cm)

Autumn yellow

Pinkish turning bronze, late summer

Sun to shade; ordinary garden conditions

Single, mass planting, flower arrangements

Clumping

Calamagrostis x acutiflora 'Karl Foerster'
(feather reed grass)

Pronunciation	kal-ah-mah-GROS-tis ah-KYOO-tih-flor-ah
Zone	4–9
Form	Medium, upright divergent
Size	Foliage 30" (75 cm) Flower 4' (1.2 m) Width 30" (75 cm)
Finest seasonal colour	Spring to summer green foliage with purple flower in summer
Flower colour & timing	Pinkish turning bronze, summer
Growing conditions	Sun; ordinary garden conditions
Landscape use	Single, mass planting, flower arrangements, screen
Growth habit	Clumping

Calamagrostis x acutiflora 'Overdam'
(feather reed grass)

Pronunciation	kal-ah-mah-GROS-tis ah-KYOO-tih-flor-ah
Zone	4–9
Form	Medium, upright divergent
Size	Foliage 30" (76 cm) Flower 4' (1.2 m) Width 30" (76 cm)
Finest seasonal colour	Spring to summer white variegated
Flower colour & timing	Pinkish turning bronze, summer
Growing conditions	Sun; ordinary garden conditions
Landscape use	Single, mass planting, flower arrangements, screen
Growth habit	Clumping

grasses at a glance

Pronunciation	**Carex albula 'Frosty Curls'**
Zone	(hair sedge)
Form	
Size	KAIR-ex ahl-BYOO-lay

Carex albula 'Frosty Curls'
(hair sedge)

Pronunciation KAIR-ex ahl-BYOO-lay
Zone 5–9
Form Small, mounded
Size Foliage 1' (30 cm) Width 14" (36 cm)
Finest seasonal colour Summer lime green
Flower colour & timing Inconspicuous flowers, June through August
Growing conditions Sun to shade; ordinary garden conditions
Landscape use Single, mass planting
Growth habit Clumping

Carex bergrenii
(bergrenii carex)

Pronunciation KAIR-ex BER-gre-NE-eye
Zone 5–9
Form Small, mounded
Size Foliage 4" (10 cm) Width 14" (36 cm)
Finest seasonal colour Summer bronze
Flower colour & timing Inconspicuous flowers, June through August
Growing conditions Sun to shade; ordinary garden conditions to moist
Landscape use Single, mass planting
Growth habit Moderately invasive

Carex buchananii
(leather leaf sedge)

Pronunciation	KAIR-ex byoo-kah-NAN-ee-eye
Zone	5–9
Form	Small, upright divergent
Size	Foliage 2' (60 cm) Width 14" (36 cm)
Finest seasonal colour	Summer bronze
Flower colour & timing	Inconspicuous flowers, June through August
Growing conditions	Sun to shade; ordinary garden conditions to moist
Landscape use	Single, mass planting, mosaic
Growth habit	Clumping

Carex buchananii 'Viridis'
(leather leaf sedge)

Pronunciation	KAIR-ex byoo-kah-NAN-ee-eye
Zone	5–9
Form	Small, upright divergent
Size	Foliage 2' (60 cm) Width 14" (36 cm)
Finest seasonal colour	Summer lime green
Flower colour & timing	Inconspicuous flowers, June through August
Growing conditions	Sun to shade; ordinary garden conditions to moist
Landscape use	Single, mass planting, mosaic
Growth habit	Clumping

grasses at a glance

Pronunciation

Zone

Form

Size

Finest seasonal colour

Flower colour & timing

Growing conditions

Landscape use

Growth habit

Carex caryophyllea 'The Beatles'
(the Beatles)

KAIR-ex cari-o-FEEL-ee-ah

5–9

Small, mounded

Foliage 1' (30 cm) Width 14" (36 cm)

Summer green

Inconspicuous flowers, June through August

Sun to shade; ordinary garden conditions

Single, mass planting

Clumping

Pronunciation

Zone

Form

Size

Finest seasonal colour

Flower colour & timing

Growing conditions

Landscape use

Growth habit

Carex comans
(New Zealand hair sedge)

KAIR-ex KOH-manz

5–9

Small, mounded

Foliage 1' (30 cm) Width 14" (36 cm)

Summer bronze

Inconspicuous flowers, June through August

Sun to shade; ordinary garden conditions

Single, mass planting

Clumping

Carex conica 'Variegata'
(miniature variegated sedge)

Pronunciation	KAIR-ex KON-ih-kah var-ee-uh-GAH-tah
Zone	5–9
Form	Small, mounded
Size	Foliage 6" (15 cm) Width 8" (20 cm)
Finest seasonal colour	Spring to summer silvery white variegation
Flower colour & timing	Inconspicuous flowers, June through August
Growing conditions	Sun to shade; ordinary garden conditions
Landscape use	Single, groundcover, mass planting
Growth habit	Clumping

Carex dolichostachya 'Kaga Nishiki'
(golden fountains)

Pronunciation	KAIR-ex
Zone	5–9
Form	Small, mounded
Size	Foliage 1' (30 cm) Width 14" (36 cm)
Finest seasonal colour	Spring to summer yellow variegated
Flower colour & timing	Inconspicuous flowers, June through August
Growing conditions	Shade to sun; ordinary garden conditions
Landscape use	Single, mass planting, mosaic, groundcover
Growth habit	Clumping

grasses at a glance

Carex elata 'Bowles' Golden'
(yellow sedge)

Pronunciation	KAIR-ex eh-LAH-tah
Zone	5–9
Form	Small, arching
Size	Foliage 18" (45 cm) Width 14" (36 cm)
Finest seasonal colour	Spring to summer yellow
Flower colour & timing	Brownish, June–July
Growing conditions	Shade; ordinary garden conditions to moist
Landscape use	Single, mosaic, mass planting
Growth habit	Clumping

Carex flacca (glaucus)
(blue sedge)

Pronunciation	KAIR-ex FLAH-kah
Zone	5–9
Form	Small, mounded
Size	Foliage 1' (30 cm) Width 2' (60 cm)
Finest seasonal colour	Spring to summer blue-green
Flower colour & timing	Inconspicuous flowers, June through August
Growing conditions	Shade to sun; ordinary garden conditions
Landscape use	Single, mass planting, mosaic, groundcover
Growth habit	Invasive

Carex japonica
(Japanese sedge)

Pronunciation	KAIR-ex jap-ON-ik-a
Zone	5–9
Form	Small, mounded
Size	Foliage 10" (25 cm) Width 2' (60 cm)
Finest seasonal colour	Spring to summer green
Flower colour & timing	Blackish, June
Growing conditions	Shade to sun; ordinary garden conditions
Landscape use	Single, mass planting, groundcover
Growth habit	Clumping

Carex morrowii 'Fishers Form'
(Fishers carex)

Pronunciation	KAIR-ex
Zone	5–9
Form	Small, mounded
Size	Foliage 1' (30 cm) Width 14" (36 cm)
Finest seasonal colour	Spring to summer yellow variegated
Flower colour & timing	Inconspicuous flowers, June through August
Growing conditions	Shade to sun; ordinary garden conditions
Landscape use	Single, mass planting, mosaic, groundcover
Growth habit	Clumping

grasses at a glance

Carex morrowii 'Ice Dance'
(ice dance sedge)

Pronunciation	KAIR-ex mor-ROH-ee-eye
Zone	5–9
Form	Small, mounded
Size	Foliage 1' (30 cm) Width 14" (36 cm)
Finest seasonal colour	Spring to summer white variegated
Flower colour & timing	Inconspicuous flowers, June through August
Growing conditions	Shade to sun; ordinary garden conditions
Landscape use	Single, mass planting, mosaic, groundcover
Growth habit	Moderately invasive

Carex oshimensis 'Evergold'
(silver variegated Japanese sedge)

Pronunciation	KAIR-ex osh-ee-MEN-sis
Zone	5–9
Form	Small, mounded
Size	Foliage 1' (30 cm) Width 14" (36 cm)
Finest seasonal colour	Spring to summer yellow variegated
Flower colour & timing	Inconspicuous flowers, June through August
Growing conditions	Shade to sun; ordinary garden conditions
Landscape use	Single, mass planting, mosaic, groundcover
Growth habit	Clumping

Carex muskingumensis
(palm sedge)

Pronunciation	KAIR-ex mus-kin-goo-MEN-sis
Zone	4–9
Form	Medium, upright arching
Size	Foliage 2' (60 cm) Width 35" (89 cm)
Finest seasonal colour	Spring to summer green
Flower colour & timing	Greenish, May–June
Growing conditions	Sun to shade; ordinary garden conditions to moist
Landscape use	Single, mass planting, groundcover, naturalizing
Growth habit	Moderately invasive

Carex pendula
(fringe sedge)

Pronunciation	KAIR-ex PEN-dyoo-lah
Zone	5–9
Form	Medium, upright arching
Size	Foliage 4' (1.2 m) Flower 5' (1.5 m) Width 4' (1.2 m)
Finest seasonal colour	Spring to summer green
Flower colour & timing	Brownish, July–August
Growing conditions	Sun to shade; ordinary garden conditions to moist
Landscape use	Single, mass planting, groundcover, naturalizing
Growth habit	Clumping

grasses at a glance

Carex plantaginea	
(plantain leafed sedge)	
Pronunciation	KAIR-ex plan-ta-jin-EE-ah
Zone	4–9
Form	Small, mounding
Size	Foliage 1' (30 cm) Width 1' (30 cm)
Finest seasonal colour	Summer green
Flower colour & timing	Inconspicuous flowers, April–May
Growing conditions	Shade; ordinary garden conditions to dry
Landscape use	Single, mass planting, groundcover, naturalizing
Growth habit	Clumping

Carex siderosticha 'Island Brocade'	
(creeping golden variegated broad-leafed sedge)	
Pronunciation	KAIR-ex sih-der-OH-stih-kah
Zone	5–9
Form	Small, mounding
Size	Foliage 1' (30 cm) Width 1' (30 cm)
Finest seasonal colour	Summer green and gold variegated
Flower colour & timing	Inconspicuous flowers, June through August
Growing conditions	Shade; ordinary garden conditions to moist
Landscape use	Single, mass planting, groundcover, naturalizing
Growth habit	Moderately invasive

Carex siderosticha 'Variegata'
(creeping variegated broad-leafed sedge)

Pronunciation	KAIR-ex sih-der-OH-stih-kah var-ee-uh-GAH-tah
Zone	5–9
Form	Small, mounding
Size	Foliage 1' (30 cm) Width 1' (30 cm)
Finest seasonal colour	Summer green and white variegated
Flower colour & timing	Brownish black, June–July
Growing conditions	Shade; ordinary garden conditions to moist
Landscape use	Single, mass planting, groundcover, naturalizing
Growth habit	Moderately invasive

Chasmanthium latifolium
(northern sea oats)

Pronunciation	kas-MAN-thee-um lat-ih-FOL-ee-um
Zone	5–9
Form	Medium, upright arching
Size	Foliage 35" (89 cm) Flower 4' (1.2 m) Width 2' (60 cm)
Finest seasonal colour	Autumn bright yellow
Flower colour & timing	Green turning copper, June–September–winter
Growing conditions	Sun to shade; ordinary garden conditions to dry
Landscape use	Single, naturalizing, flower arrangements, mass planting
Growth habit	Clumping

grasses at a glance

Cortaderia selloana
(pampas grass)

Pronunciation	kor-tah-DEER-ee-ah sell-oh-AN-ah
Zone	8–10
Form	Tall, upright arching
Size	Foliage 5' (1.5 m) Flower 8' (2.5 m) Width 5' (1.5 m)
Finest seasonal colour	Late summer green
Flower colour & timing	Pink or white; August–September–winter
Growing conditions	Sun; ordinary garden conditions
Landscape use	Single, mass planting
Growth habit	Clumping

Deschampsia cespitosa
(tufted hair grass)

Pronunciation	deh-SHAMP-see-ah ses-pih-TOH-sah
Zone	3–8
Form	Medium, mounded
Size	Foliage 16" (40 cm) Flower 42" (106 cm) Width 35" (89 cm)
Finest seasonal colour	Summer green
Flower colour & timing	Yellow to gold, May–June
Growing conditions	Sun to shade; ordinary garden conditions
Landscape use	Single, mass planting
Growth habit	Clumping

Deschampsia cespitosa 'Northern Lights'
(variegated tufted hair grass)

Pronunciation	deh-SHAMP-see-ah ses-pih-TOH-sah
Zone	4–8
Form	Small, mounded
Size	Foliage 10" (25 cm) Width 14" (36 cm)
Finest seasonal colour	Summer white and green variegated
Flower colour & timing	Yellow to gold, May–June
Growing conditions	Sun to shade; ordinary garden conditions
Landscape use	Single, mass planting
Growth habit	Clumping

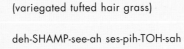

Eragrostis trichodes
(love grass)

Pronunciation	air-ah-GROS-tis trih-KOH-deez
Zone	5–9
Form	Medium, mounded
Size	Foliage 2' (60 cm) Flower 3' (90 cm) Width 3' (90 cm)
Finest seasonal colour	Summer green
Flower colour & timing	Amethyst pink, late July
Growing conditions	Sun; well-drained soil
Landscape use	Single, mass planting
Growth habit	Clumping

grasses at a glance

Pronunciation	
Zone	
Form	
Size	
Finest seasonal colour	
Flower colour & timing	
Growing conditions	
Landscape use	
Growth habit	

Eriophorum angustifolium
(cotton grass)

air-ee-OH-for-um an-gus-tif-OL-e-um

4–7

Medium, arching

Foliage 1' (30 cm) Flower 2' (60 cm) Width 2' (60 cm)

Spring flowers white cottony heads

White, May

Sun; ordinary garden conditions to moist

Single, mass planting, containers

Clumping

Pronunciation	
Zone	
Form	
Size	
Finest seasonal colour	
Flower colour & timing	
Growing conditions	
Landscape use	
Growth habit	

Festuca amethystina 'Superba'
(rainbow fescue)

fes-TOO-kah am-eh-this-TEE-nah

4–8

Medium, tufted

Foliage 1' (30 cm) Flower 2' (60 cm) Width 18" (46 cm)

Summer blue foliage with rainbow-coloured stems

Purplish, May–June

Sun; ordinary garden conditions to dry

Single, mass planting

Clumping

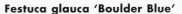

Festuca glauca 'Boulder Blue'
(blue fescue)

Pronunciation	fes-TOO-kah GLOU-kah
Zone	4–9
Form	Small, tufted
Size	Foliage 1' (30 cm) Flower 14" (36 cm) Width 14" (36 cm)
Finest seasonal colour	Spring to summer powder blue
Flower colour & timing	Bluish, May–June
Growing conditions	Sun; ordinary garden conditions to dry
Landscape use	Single, mosaic, mass planting
Growth habit	Clumping

Festuca glauca 'Elijah Blue' 'Sea Urchin'
(sea urchin fescue)

Pronunciation	fes-TOO-kah GLOU-kah
Zone	4–9
Form	Small, tufted
Size	Foliage 1' (30 cm) Flower 14" (36 cm) Width 14" (36 cm)
Finest seasonal colour	Spring to summer blue
Flower colour & timing	Bluish, May–June
Growing conditions	Sun; ordinary garden conditions
Landscape use	Single, mosaic, mass planting
Growth habit	Clumping

grasses at a glance

Festuca ovina glauca
(blue fescue)

Pronunciation	fes-TOO-kah oh-VEE-nah GLOU-kah
Zone	4–9
Form	Small, tufted
Size	**Foliage** 1' (30 cm) **Flower** 18" (45 cm) **Width** 18" (45 cm)
Finest seasonal colour	**Spring to summer** blue
Flower colour & timing	Bluish, May–June
Growing conditions	Sun; ordinary garden conditions
Landscape use	Single, mosaic, mass planting
Growth habit	Clumping

Glyceria maxima 'Variegata'
(Variegated manna grass)

Pronunciation	GLIH-seer-ee-ah MAX-ih-mah var-ee-uh-GAH-tah
Zone	5–10
Form	Medium, upright arching
Size	**Foliage** 2' (60 cm) **Flower** 30" (75 cm) **Width** 3' (90 cm)
Finest seasonal colour	**Summer** white and green variegated
Flower colour & timing	Seldom flowers
Growing conditions	Sun; ordinary garden conditions to moist
Landscape use	Single, groundcover, mosaic, mass planting
Growth habit	Moderately invasive

Hakonechloa macra
(hakone grass)

Pronunciation	hah-koh-neh-KLOH-ah MAK-rah
Zone	5–9
Form	Small, mounded
Size	Foliage 1' (30 cm) Width 2' (60 cm)
Finest seasonal colour	Summer green Autumn/Winter brilliant bronze
Flower colour & timing	Light bronze, late summer
Growing conditions	Shade; ordinary garden conditions
Landscape use	Single, groundcover, mosaic, mass planting
Growth habit	Clumping

Hakonechloa macra 'Aureola'
(golden variegated hakone grass)

Pronunciation	hah-koh-neh-KLOH-ah MAK-rah aw-ree-OH-la
Zone	5–9
Form	Small, mounded
Size	Foliage 1' (30 cm) Width 2' (60 cm)
Finest seasonal colour	Spring to summer yellow variegated
Flower colour & timing	Light bronze, late summer
Growing conditions	Shade; ordinary garden conditions
Landscape use	Single, groundcover, containers
Growth habit	Clumping

grasses at a glance

Pronunciation

Zone

Form

Size

Finest seasonal colour

Flower colour & timing

Growing conditions

Landscape use

Growth habit

Helictotrichon sempervirens
(blue oat grass)

hel-ik-toh-TREE-kon sem-per-VEYE-renz

4–8

Medium, mounded

Foliage 16" (40 cm) Flower 46" (1.2 m) Width 2' (60 cm)

Spring to summer winter blue

Golden, June

Sun to part shade; ordinary garden conditions to dry

Single, mosaic, mass planting

Clumping

Pronunciation

Zone

Form

Size

Finest seasonal colour

Flower colour & timing

Growing conditions

Landscape use

Growth habit

Holcus mollis 'Albo-variegatus'
(variegated velvet grass)

HOL-kus MOL-us AL-bo var-ee-uh-GAH-tus

5–8

Small, mounded

Foliage 6" (15 cm) Width 1' (30 cm)

Spring to summer white variegated

White, June

Part shade; ordinary garden conditions

Single, mosaic, mass planting, groundcover

Moderately invasive

Hordeum jubatum
(foxtail barley)

Pronunciation	hor-DEE-um joo-BAH-tum
Zone	4–7
Form	Medium, arching
Size	Foliage 18" (45 cm) Flower 2' (60 cm) Width 2' (60 cm)
Finest seasonal colour	Spring to summer green
Flower colour & timing	light purple, June
Growing conditions	Sun; ordinary garden conditions
Landscape use	Single, naturalizing, mass planting, flower arrangements
Growth habit	Clumping

Hystrix patula
(bottlebrush grass)

Pronunciation	HEYE-striks pah-TOO-lah
Zone	4–7
Form	Medium, arching
Size	Foliage 1' (30 cm) Flower 2' (60 cm) Width 2' (60 cm)
Finest seasonal colour	Summer green
Flower colour & timing	Greenish, June
Growing conditions	Shade; ordinary garden conditions to dry
Landscape use	Single, naturalizing, flower arrangements, mass planting
Growth habit	Clumping

grasses at a glance

Imperata cylindrica 'Red Baron'
(Japanese blood grass)

Pronunciation	im-per-AH-tah
Zone	5–9
Form	Small, upright erect
Size	Foliage 16" (40 cm) Width 18" (45 cm)
Finest seasonal colour	Spring to summer and autumn blood red
Flower colour & timing	Does not produce flowers
Growing conditions	Sun; ordinary garden conditions to moist
Landscape use	Single, groundcover, containers, mass planting
Growth habit	Moderately invasive

Koeleria glauca
(large blue hair grass)

Pronunciation	koh-LAIR-ee-ah GLOU-kah
Zone	4–8
Form	Small, tufted
Size	Foliage 1' (30 cm) Width 18" (45 cm)
Finest seasonal colour	Spring to summer blue
Flower colour & timing	Blue-green, May–June
Growing conditions	Sun; ordinary garden conditions
Landscape use	Single, mass planting, naturalizing
Growth habit	Clumping

Leymus arenarius 'Glauca'
(blue lyme rye)

Pronunciation	Lee-mus ar-EEN-arus GLOU-kus
Zone	4–9
Form	Medium, arching
Size	Foliage 30" (75 cm) Flower 42" (106 cm) Width 2' (60 cm)
Finest seasonal colour	Spring to summer blue
Flower colour & timing	Bronze, June–July
Growing conditions	Sun; ordinary garden conditions to dry
Landscape use	Single, containers, mass planting, erosion control
Growth habit	Invasive

Luzula nivea
(snowy woodrush)

Pronunciation	loo-ZOO-lah NIV-ee-ah
Zone	4–9
Form	Small, tufted
Size	Foliage 8" (20 cm) Flower 1' (30 cm) Width 1' (30 cm)
Finest seasonal colour	Spring to summer green
Flower colour & timing	White flowers, May–June
Growing conditions	Sun to shade; ordinary garden conditions
Landscape use	Single, mass planting
Growth habit	Clumping

grasses at a glance

Pronunciation	**Luzula sylvatica** (greater woodrush)
	loo-ZOO-lah sill-VAH-tee-kah
Zone	4–9
Form	Small, tufted
Size	Foliage 8" (20 cm) Flower 1' (30 cm) Width 1' (30 cm)
Finest seasonal colour	Spring to summer, green leaves
Flower colour & timing	Yellow green flowers, May–June
Growing conditions	Sun to shade; ordinary garden conditions
Landscape use	Single, mass planting
Growth habit	Clumping

Pronunciation	**Milium effusum 'Aureum'** (golden wood millet)
	MIL-ee-um eh-FYOO-sum AW-ree-um
Zone	5–9
Form	Small, tufted
Size	Foliage 1' (30 cm) Flower 2' (60 cm) Width 2' (60 cm)
Finest seasonal colour	Summer yellow
Flower colour & timing	Golden yellow; May–June
Growing conditions	Part shade; ordinary garden conditions to moist
Landscape use	Single, mass planting
Growth habit	Loosely clumping

Miscanthus floridulus
(Siberian bamboo)

Pronunciation	mis-KAN-thus FLO-rid-UL-us
Zone	4–9
Form	Tall, upright arching
Size	Foliage 14' (4.2 m) Flower 15' (4.6 m) Width 6' (2 m)
Finest seasonal colour	Autumn blonde
Flower colour & timing	Rarely flowers, late November
Growing conditions	Sun; ordinary garden conditions to moist
Landscape use	Single, mass planting, screen
Growth habit	Moderately invasive

Miscanthus purpurascens
(flame grass)

Pronunciation	mis-KAN-thus pur-pur-AH-senz
Zone	4–9
Form	Tall, upright arching
Size	Foliage 4' (1.2 m) Flower 5' (1.5 m) Width 3' (90 cm)
Finest seasonal colour	Autumn red
Flower colour & timing	White, September
Growing conditions	Sun; ordinary garden conditions
Landscape use	Single, mosaic, mass planting, flower arrangements
Growth habit	Clumping

grasses at a glance

Miscanthus sinensis 'Arabesque'	
(maiden grass)	
Pronunciation	mis-KAN-thus sin-EN-sis
Zone	4–9
Form	Medium, upright arching
Size	Foliage 4' (1.2 m) Flower 5' (1.5 m) Width 3' (90 cm)
Finest seasonal colour	Summer to autumn blonde
Flower colour & timing	Pink turning white, September
Growing conditions	Sun; ordinary garden conditions
Landscape use	Single, mosaic, mass planting, flower arrangements
Growth habit	Clumping

Miscanthus sinensis 'Berlin'	
(Japanese silver grass)	
Pronunciation	mis-KAN-thus sin-EN-sis
Zone	5–9
Form	Tall, upright arching
Size	Foliage 6' (1.8 m) Flower 7' (2.1 m) Width 5' (1.5 m)
Finest seasonal colour	Spring to summer green
Flower colour & timing	Golden, September
Growing conditions	Sun; ordinary garden conditions to dry
Landscape use	Single, mass planting, flower arrangements
Growth habit	Clumping

Miscanthus sinensis 'Cabaret'
(Japanese silver grass)

Pronunciation	mis-KAN-thus sin-EN-sis
Zone	6–9
Form	Tall, upright arching
Size	Foliage 5' (1.5 m) flower 6' (1.8 m) width 5' (1.5 m)
Finest seasonal colour	Autumn white variegated
Flower colour & timing	Copper, October–November
Growing conditions	Sun; ordinary garden conditions
Landscape use	Single, mosaic, mass planting
Growth habit	Clumping

Miscanthus sinensis 'Gracillimus'
(maiden grass)

Pronunciation	mis-KAN-thus sin-EN-sis gra-SILL-ih-mus
Zone	5–9
Form	Tall, upright arching
Size	Foliage 5' (1.5 m) Flower 6' (1.8 m) Width 5' (1.5m)
Finest seasonal colour	Winter blonde
Flower colour & timing	Copper, November
Growing conditions	Sun; ordinary garden conditions
Landscape use	Single, mass planting, flower arrangements
Growth habit	Clumping

grasses at a glance

Pronunciation

Zone

Form

Size

Finest seasonal colour

Flower colour & timing

Growing conditions

Landscape use

Growth habit

Miscanthus sinensis 'Graziella'
(Japanese silver grass)

mis-KAN-thus sin-EN-sis

5–9

Tall, upright arching

Foliage 5' (1.5 m) Flower 6' (1.8 m) Width 5' (1.5 m)

Autumn to winter blonde

White, September

Sun; ordinary garden conditions

Single, mass planting, flower arrangements

Clumping

Pronunciation

Zone

Form

Size

Finest seasonal colour

Flower colour & timing

Growing conditions

Landscape use

Growth habit

Miscanthus sinensis 'Grosse Fontaine'
(large fountain Japanese silver grass)

mis-KAN-thus sin-EN-sis

5–9

Tall, upright arching

Foliage 6' (1.8 m) Flower 8' (2.4 m) Width 6' (1.8 m)

Winter blonde

Pink, September

Sun; ordinary garden conditions

Single, mass planting, flower arrangements

Clumping

Miscanthus sinensis 'Huron Blush'
(Huron maiden grass)

Pronunciation	mis-KAN-thus sin-EN-sis
Zone	4–9
Form	Medium, upright arching
Size	Foliage 3' (90 cm) Flower 4' (1.2 m) Width 3' (90 cm)
Finest seasonal colour	Summer green Winter blonde
Flower colour & timing	Blush pink, September
Growing conditions	Sun; ordinary garden conditions
Landscape use	Single, mass planting, flower arrangements, mosaic
Growth habit	Clumping

Miscanthus sinensis 'Huron Penetangore'
(big dot)

Pronunciation	mis-KAN-thus sin-EN-sis
Zone	4–9
Form	Tall, upright arching
Size	Foliage 5' (1.5 m) Flower 6' (1.8 m) Width 5' (1.5 m)
Finest seasonal colour	Spring to summer yellow variegated
Flower colour & timing	Pink, September–October
Growing conditions	Sun; ordinary garden conditions
Landscape use	Single, mass planting, flower arrangements, screen
Growth habit	Clumping

grasses at a glance

Miscanthus sinensis 'Huron Sentinel'
(maiden grass)

Pronunciation	mis-KAN-thus sin-EN-sis
Zone	4–9
Form	Tall, upright arching
Size	Foliage 5' (1.5 m) Flower 6' (2 m) Width 5' (1.5 m)
Finest seasonal colour	Summer green Winter blonde
Flower colour & timing	Bronze, late September
Growing conditions	Sun; ordinary garden conditions
Landscape use	Single, mass planting, flower arrangements, mosaic
Growth habit	Clumping

Miscanthus sinensis 'Huron Sunrise'
(Huron maiden grass)

Pronunciation	mis-KAN-thus sin-EN-sis
Zone	4–9
Form	Tall, upright arching
Size	Foliage 4' (1.2 m) Flower 5' (1.5 m) Width 4' (1.2 m)
Finest seasonal colour	Summer green Winter blonde
Flower colour & timing	Burgundy, August
Growing conditions	Sun; ordinary garden conditions
Landscape use	Single, mass planting, flower arrangements, mosaic
Growth habit	Clumping

Miscanthus sinensis 'Huron Sunset'
(maiden grass)

Pronunciation	mis-KAN-thus sin-EN-sis
Zone	4–9
Form	Medium, upright arching
Size	Foliage 3' (90 cm) Flower 4' (1.2 m) Width 3' (90 cm)
Finest seasonal colour	Summer green Winter blonde
Flower colour & timing	Burgundy, August
Growing conditions	Sun; ordinary garden conditions
Landscape use	Single, mass planting, flower arrangements, mosaic
Growth habit	Clumping

Miscanthus sinensis 'Little Zebra'
(little zebra grass)

Pronunciation	mis-KAN-thus sin-EN-sis
Zone	4–9
Form	Medium, upright arching
Size	Foliage 2' (60 cm) Flower 3' (90 cm) Width 3' (90 cm)
Finest seasonal colour	Autumn blonde, yellow and green variegated
Flower colour & timing	Pink, September–October
Growing conditions	Sun; ordinary garden conditions
Landscape use	Single, mosaic, mass planting, flower arrangements
Growth habit	Clumping

grasses at a glance

Pronunciation

Zone

Form

Size

Finest seasonal colour

Flower colour & timing

Growing conditions

Landscape use

Growth habit

Miscanthus sinensis 'Malepartus'
(large fountain Japanese silver grass)

mis-KAN-thus sin-EN-sis

4–9

Tall, upright arching

Foliage 6' (1.8 m) Flower 7' (2.1 m) Width 5' (1.5 m)

Winter blonde

Pink, August

Sun; ordinary garden conditions

Single, mass planting, flower arrangements

Clumping

Pronunciation

Zone

Form

Size

Finest seasonal colour

Flower colour & timing

Growing conditions

Landscape use

Growth habit

Miscanthus sinensis 'Morning Light'
(miniature variegated grass)

mis-KAN-thus sin-EN-sis

4–9

Medium, upright arching

Foliage 4' (1.2 m) Flower 4' (1.2 m) Width 3' (90 cm)

Summer white and green variegated Autumn blonde

Bronze, November

Sun; ordinary garden conditions

Single, mosaic, mass planting, flower arrangements

Clumping

Miscanthus sinensis 'Puenktchen'
(little dot)

Pronunciation	mis-KAN-thus sin-EN-sis
Zone	4–9
Form	Tall, upright arching
Size	Foliage 4' (1.2 m) Flower 5' (1.5 m) Width 3' (90 cm)
Finest seasonal colour	Autumn blonde, yellow and green variegated
Flower colour & timing	Pinkish, September–October
Growing conditions	Sun; ordinary garden conditions
Landscape use	Single, mosaic, mass planting, flower arrangements
Growth habit	Clumping

Miscanthus sinensis 'Sacchariflorus'
(silver banner grass)

Pronunciation	mis-KAN-thus sak-kar-ih-FLOR-us
Zone	4–9
Form	Tall, upright arching
Size	Foliage 5' (1.5 m) Flower 6' (2 m) Width 5' (1.5 m)
Finest seasonal colour	Winter blonde
Flower colour & timing	White, September
Growing conditions	Sun; ordinary garden conditions
Landscape use	Single, mass planting, flower arrangements
Growth habit	Invasive

grasses at a glance

Miscanthus sinensis 'Sarabande'
(Japanese silver grass)

Pronunciation	mis-KAN-thus sin-EN-sis
Zone	4–9
Form	Tall, upright arching
Size	Foliage 4' (1.2 m) Flower 5' (1.5 m) Width 3' (90 cm)
Finest seasonal colour	Autumn blonde
Flower colour & timing	White, September
Growing conditions	Sun; ordinary garden conditions
Landscape use	Single, mosaic, mass planting, flower arrangements
Growth habit	Clumping

Miscanthus sinensis 'Silberfeder'
(silver feather maiden grass)

Pronunciation	mis-KAN-thus sin-EN-sis
Zone	4–9
Form	Tall, upright arching
Size	Foliage 6' (1.8 m) Flower 7' (2.1 m) Width 5' (1.5 m)
Finest seasonal colour	Winter blonde
Flower colour & timing	White, September
Growing conditions	Sun; ordinary garden conditions
Landscape use	Single, mass planting, flower arrangements
Growth habit	Clumping

Miscanthus sinensis 'Strictus'
(porcupine grass)

Pronunciation	mis-KAN-thus sin-EN-sis STRIK-tus
Zone	4–9
Form	Tall, upright arching
Size	Foliage 5' (1.5 m) Flower 6' (1.8 m) Width 4' (1.2 m)
Finest seasonal colour	Spring to summer yellow variegated
Flower colour & timing	Bronze, October
Growing conditions	Sun; ordinary garden conditions to moist
Landscape use	Single, mass planting, flower arrangements
Growth habit	Clumping

Miscanthus sinensis 'Variegatus'
(variegated Japanese silver grass)

Pronunciation	mis-KAN-thus sin-EN-sis var-ee-uh-GAH-tus
Zone	4–9
Form	Tall, upright arching
Size	Foliage 5' (1.5 m) Flower 6' (1.8 m) Width 5' (1.5 m)
Finest seasonal colour	Summer and autumn white variegated
Flower colour & timing	Bronze, November
Growing conditions	Sun; ordinary garden conditions
Landscape use	Single, mass planting, flower arrangements
Growth habit	Clumping

grasses at a glance

Pronunciation

Zone

Form

Size

Finest seasonal colour

Flower colour & timing

Growing conditions

Landscape use

Growth habit

Miscanthus sinensis 'Yaku Jima'
(Yaku Jima Japanese silver grass)

mis-KAN-thus sin-EN-sis YAH-koo JEE-mah

4–9

Tall, upright arching

Foliage 4' (1.2 m) Flower 5' (1.5 m) Width 3' (90 cm)

Autumn blonde, leaves are fine textured

Pinkish, October

Sun; ordinary garden conditions

Single, mosaic, mass planting, flower arrangements

Clumping

Pronunciation

Zone

Form

Size

Finest seasonal colour

Flower colour & timing

Growing conditions

Landscape use

Growth habit

Miscanthus sinensis 'Zebrinus'
(zebra grass)

mis-KAN-thus sin-EN-sis zeh-BREYE-nus

4–9

Tall, upright arching

Foliage 5' (1.5 m) Flower 6' (1.8 m) Width 5' (1.5 m)

Spring to summer yellow variegated

Pinkish, late September–early October

Sun; ordinary garden conditions

Single, mass planting; flower arrangements, screen

Clumping

Molinia caerulea ssp. **arundinacea 'Skyracer'**
(tall purple moor grass)

Pronunciation	moh-LIN-ee-ah se-RU-le-a
Zone	4–8
Form	Tall upright divergent
Size	Foliage 3' (90 cm) Flower 8' (2.4 m) Width 6' (1.8 m)
Finest seasonal colour	Autumn blonde
Flower colour & timing	Purplish turning light bronze, July–August
Growing conditions	Sun; ordinary garden conditions to moist
Landscape use	Single, mass planting
Growth habit	Clumping

Molinia caerulea 'Heidebraut'
(moor grass)

Pronunciation	moh-LIN-ee-ah ser-OO-lee-ah
Zone	4–8
Form	Medium, upright divergent
Size	Foliage 1' (60 cm) Flower 3' (90 cm) Width 2' (60 cm)
Finest seasonal colour	Autumn blonde
Flower colour & timing	Purplish turning light bronze, July–August
Growing conditions	Sun to shade; ordinary garden conditions
Landscape use	Single, containers, mass planting
Growth habit	Clumping

grasses at a glance

Molinia caerulea 'Moorhexe'
(purple moor grass)

Pronunciation	moh-LIN-ee-ah ser-OO-lee-ah
Zone	4–8
Form	Medium, upright divergent
Size	Foliage 1' (30 cm) Flower 3' (90 cm) Width 2' (60 cm)
Finest seasonal colour	Autumn blonde
Flower colour & timing	Purplish turning light bronze, July–August
Growing conditions	Sun to shade; ordinary garden conditions
Landscape use	Single, containers, mass planting
Growth habit	Clumping

Molinia caerulea 'Variegata'
(variegated moor grass)

Pronunciation	moh-LIN-ee-ah ser-OO-lee-ah ver-ee-uh-GAH-tah
Zone	4–8
Form	Medium, arching
Size	Foliage 18" (45 cm) Flower 30" (75 cm) Width 2' (60 cm)
Finest seasonal colour	Spring to summer yellow variegated
Flower colour & timing	Golden, July–August
Growing conditions	Sun to shade; ordinary garden conditions
Landscape use	Single, containers, mass planting
Growth habit	Clumping

Panicum virgatum
(switch grass)

Pronunciation	PAN-ih-kum veer-GAH-tum
Zone	4–9
Form	Medium, arching
Size	Foliage 3' (90 cm) Flower 4' (1.2 m) Width 4' (1.2 m)
Finest seasonal colour	Autumn yellow
Flower colour & timing	Pinkish turning brown, July–August
Growing conditions	Sun; ordinary garden conditions to moist
Landscape use	Single, mass planting, naturalizing
Growth habit	Clumping

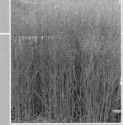

Panicum virgatum 'Heavy Metal'
(blue switch grass)

Pronunciation	PAN-ih-kum veer-GAH-tum
Zone	4–9
Form	Tall, upright erect
Size	Foliage 3' (90 cm) Flower 4' (1.2 m) Width 3' (90 cm)
Finest seasonal colour	Spring to summer blue Autumn and winter red/blonde
Flower colour & timing	Pinkish turning brown, July–August
Growing conditions	Sun; ordinary garden conditions
Landscape use	Single, mass planting
Growth habit	Clumping

grasses at a glance

Panicum virgatum 'Huron Solstice'
(Huron switch grass)

Pronunciation	PAN-ih-kum veer-GAH-tum
Zone	4–9
Form	Medium, upright erect
Size	Foliage 3' (90 cm) Flower 4' (1.2 m) Width 3' (90 cm)
Finest seasonal colour	Spring to summer burgundy Autumn and winter red/blonde
Flower colour & timing	Pinkish turning brown, July–August
Growing conditions	Sun; ordinary garden conditions
Landscape use	Single, mass planting
Growth habit	Clumping

Panicum virgatum 'Prairie Sky'
(blue switch grass)

Pronunciation	PAN-ih-kum veer-GAH-tum
Zone	4–9
Form	Medium, upright erect
Size	Foliage 3' (90 cm) Flower 4' (1.2 m) Width 3' (90 cm)
Finest seasonal colour	Spring to summer blue Autumn and winter red/blonde
Flower colour & timing	Pinkish turning brown, July–August
Growing conditions	Sun; ordinary garden conditions
Landscape use	Single, mass planting
Growth habit	Clumping

Panicum virgatum 'Rehbraun'
(switch grass)

Pronunciation	PAN-ih-kum veer-GAH-tum
Zone	4–9
Form	Medium, arching
Size	Foliage 3' (90 cm) Flower 4' (1.2 m) Width 4' (1.2 m)
Finest seasonal colour	Autumn to winter red
Flower colour & timing	Pinkish turning brown, July–August
Growing conditions	Sun; ordinary garden conditions
Landscape use	Single, mass planting
Growth habit	Clumping

Panicum virgatum 'Shenandoah'
(switch grass)

Pronunciation	PAN-ih-kum veer-GAH-tum
Zone	4–9
Form	Medium, arching
Size	Foliage 3' (90 cm) Flower 4' (1.2 m) Width 4' (1.2 m)
Finest seasonal colour	Summer to autumn red
Flower colour & timing	Purplish turning brown, July–August
Growing conditions	Sun; ordinary garden conditions
Landscape use	Single, mass planting
Growth habit	Clumping

grasses at a glance

Pronunciation

Zone

Form

Size

Finest seasonal colour

Flower colour & timing

Growing conditions

Landscape use

Growth habit

Panicum virgatum 'Warrior'
(switch grass)

PAN-ih-kum veer-GAH-tum

4–9

Medium, arching

Foliage 3' (90 cm) Flower 4' (1.2 m) Width 4' (1.2 m)

Autumn to winter red

Purplish turning brown, July–August

Sun; ordinary garden conditions

Single, mass planting

Clumping

Pronunciation

Zone

Form

Size

Finest seasonal colour

Flower colour & timing

Growing conditions

Landscape use

Growth habit

Pennisetum alopecuroides
(hardy fountain grass)

pen-ih-SEE-tum al-oh-pek-yur-OY-deez

5–9

Medium, arching

Foliage 30" (75 cm) Flower 3' (90 cm) Width 3' (90 cm)

Autumn and winter yellow

Pinkish, July–August

Sun; ordinary garden conditions

Single, mass planting, flower arrangements

Clumping

Pronunciation	
Zone	
Form	
Size	
Finest seasonal colour	
Flower colour & timing	
Growing conditions	
Landscape use	
Growth habit	

Pennisetum alopecuroides 'Hameln'
(miniature fountain grass)

pen-ih-SEE-tum al-oh-pek-yur-OY-deez HAH-muln

5–9

Small, arching

Foliage 18" (36 cm) Flower 2' (60 cm) Width 2' (60 cm)

Autumn to winter yellow

Whitish, July–August

Sun; ordinary garden conditions

Single, groundcover, mass planting

Clumping

Pennisetum alopecuroides 'Little Bunny'
(fountain grass)

pen-ih-SEE-tum al-oh-pek-yur-OY-deez

5–9

Small, tufted

Foliage 8" (20 cm) Flower 1' (30 cm) Width 18" (45 cm)

Spring to summer green leaves

Whitish, July–August

Sun; ordinary garden conditions

Single, mass planting

Clumping

grasses at a glance

Pennisetum alopecuroides 'Little Honey'
(fountain grass)

Pronunciation	pen-ih-SEE-tum al-oh-pek-yur-OY-deez
Zone	5–9
Form	Small, tufted
Size	Foliage 8" (20 cm) Flower 1' (30 cm) Width 18" (45 cm)
Finest seasonal colour	Spring to summer white variegated
Flower colour & timing	Whitish, July–August
Growing conditions	Sun; ordinary garden conditions
Landscape use	Single, mass planting
Growth habit	Clumping

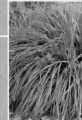

Pennisetum alopecuroides 'Moudry'
(black-flowering fountain grass)

Pronunciation	pen-ih-SEE-tum al-oh-pek-yur-OY-deez MOU-dree
Zone	5–9
Form	Medium, arching
Size	Foliage 3' (90 cm) Flower 4' (1.2 m) Width 3' (90 cm)
Finest seasonal colour	Spring to summer green
Flower colour & timing	Purplish black, September
Growing conditions	Sun to semi-shade; ordinary garden conditions
Landscape use	Single, mass planting
Growth habit	Clumping

Pennisetum glaucum
(red-leafed millet)

Pronunciation	pen-ih-SEE-tum GLOU-kum
Zone	8–10
Form	Annual, tall, arching
Size	Foliage 4' (1.2 m) Flower 5' (1.5 m) Width 2' (60 cm)
Finest seasonal colour	Spring to summer burgundy
Flower colour & timing	Burgundy, July
Growing conditions	Sun; ordinary garden conditions
Landscape use	Single, mosaic, mass plantings, flower arrangements
Growth habit	Clumping

Pennisetum messiacum 'Red Bunny Tails'
(Red Bunny Tails fountain grass)

Pronunciation	pen-ih-SEE-tum
Zone	8–10
Form	Annual, medium, arching
Size	Foliage 2' (60 cm) Flower 3' (90 cm) Width 3' (90 cm)
Finest seasonal colour	Spring to summer burgundy tones
Flower colour & timing	Blonde with a tint of red, July
Growing conditions	Sun; ordinary garden conditions
Landscape use	Single, mosaic, mass plantings, flower arrangements
Growth habit	Clumping

grasses at a glance

Pennisetum orientale
(Oriental fountain grass)

Pronunciation	pen-ih-SEE-tum or-ee-en-TAL-ee
Zone	6–9
Form	Small, arching
Size	Foliage 18" (36 cm) Flower 2' (60 cm) Width 2' (60 cm)
Finest seasonal colour	Summer to autumn early pink flowers
Flower colour & timing	Whitish, July–August
Growing conditions	Sun; ordinary garden conditions
Landscape use	Single, groundcover, mass planting
Growth habit	Clumping

Pennisetum setaceum 'Burgundy Giant'
(giant purple-leaved fountain grass)

Pronunciation	pen-ih-SEE-tum seh-TAY-see-um
Zone	8–10
Form	Annual, tall, arching
Size	Foliage 4' (1.2 m) Flower 5' (1.5 m) Width 3' (90 cm)
Finest seasonal colour	Spring to summer burgundy
Flower colour & timing	Burgundy, July–August
Growing conditions	Sun; ordinary garden conditions
Landscape use	Single, mosaic, mass plantings, flower arrangements
Growth habit	Clumping

Pennisetum setaceum 'Eaton Canyon'
(dwarf purple-leaved fountain grass)

Pronunciation	pen-ih-SEE-tum seh-TAY-see-um
Zone	8–10
Form	Annual, medium, arching
Size	Foliage 1' (30 cm) Flower 2' (60 cm) Width 2' (60 cm)
Finest seasonal colour	Spring to summer burgundy
Flower colour & timing	Burgundy, July–August
Growing conditions	Sun; ordinary garden conditions
Landscape use	Single, mosaic, mass plantings, flower arrangements
Growth habit	Clumping

Pennisetum setaceum 'Rubrum'
(purple-leaved fountain grass)

Pronunciation	pen-ih-SEE-tum seh-TAY-see-um ROO-brum
Zone	8–10
Form	Annual, medium, arching
Size	Foliage 2' (60 cm) Flower 3' (90 cm) Width 3' (90 cm)
Finest seasonal colour	Spring to summer burgundy
Flower colour & timing	Burgundy, July–August
Growing conditions	Sun; ordinary garden conditions
Landscape use	Single, mosaic, mass planting, flower arrangements
Growth habit	Clumping

grasses at a glance

Pennisetum setaceum 'Ruppelii'
(annual fountain grass)

Pronunciation	pen-ih-SEE-tum seh-TAY-see-um
Zone	8–10
Form	Annual, medium, arching
Size	Foliage 2' (60 cm) Flower 3' (90 cm) Width 3' (90 cm)
Finest seasonal colour	Spring to summer Burgundy
Flower colour & timing	Burgundy pink, July
Growing conditions	Sun; ordinary garden conditions
Landscape use	Single, mosaic, mass plantings, flower arrangements
Growth habit	Clumping

Phalaris arundinacea 'Picta'
(ribbon grass)

Pronunciation	fah-LAR-is ah-run-din-AH-see-ah
Zone	4–9
Form	Medium, upright arching
Size	Foliage 2' (60 cm) Flower 3' (90 cm) Width 3' (90 cm)
Finest seasonal colour	Summer white variegated
Flower colour & timing	White, June–July
Growing conditions	Sun to shade; ordinary garden conditions to moist
Landscape use	Single, containers, mass planting
Growth habit	Invasive

Phalaris arundinacea 'Feesey's Form'
(strawberries and cream ribbon grass)

Pronunciation	fah-LAR-is ah-run-din-AH-see-ah
Zone	4–9
Form	Medium, upright arching
Size	Foliage 2' (60 cm) Flower 3' (90 cm) Width 3' (90 cm)
Finest seasonal colour	Summer to autumn white variegated
Flower colour & timing	White, June–July
Growing conditions	Sun to shade; ordinary garden conditions to moist
Landscape use	Single, containers, mass planting
Growth habit	Invasive

Saccharum ravennae (prev. **Erianthus ravennae**)
(hardy pampas grass)

Pronunciation	sa-KAR-um ra-VEN-nay
Zone	5–9
Form	Tall, upright arching
Size	Foliage 5' (1.5 m) Flower 15' (4.6 m) Width 5' (1.5m)
Finest seasonal colour	Spring to summer green Autumn blonde
Flower colour & timing	Silvery-purple, August
Growing conditions	Sun; ordinary garden conditions
Landscape use	Single, mosaic, mass planting
Growth habit	Clumping

grasses at a glance

Pronunciation	**Schizachyrium scoparium** (little bluestem)
	skits-ah-KEER-ee-um skoh-PAIR-ee-um
Zone	4–9
Form	Medium, upright divergent
Size	Foliage 2' (60 cm) Flower 3' (90 cm) Width 2' (60 cm)
Finest seasonal colour	Autumn to winter red/bronze
Flower colour & timing	Bronze, August–September
Growing conditions	Sun; ordinary garden conditions to dry
Landscape use	Single, naturalizing, mass planting, flower arrangements
Growth habit	Clumping

	Sesleria autumnalis (autumn moor grass)
Pronunciation	sez-LAIR-ee-ah aw-TUM-nal-is
Zone	5–9
Form	Medium, arching
Size	Foliage 1' (30 cm) Flower 2' (60 cm) Width 2' (60 cm)
Finest seasonal colour	Autumn bright yellow
Flower colour & timing	Purplish-black, September
Growing conditions	Sun; ordinary garden conditions
Landscape use	Single, mass planting, naturalizing, groundcover
Growth habit	Clumping

Sorghastrum nutans 'Sioux Blue'
(Indian grass)

Pronunciation	sor-GAS-trum NOO-tanz
Zone	4–9
Form	Medium, upright arching
Size	Foliage 3' (90 cm) Flower 5' (1.5 cm) Width 3' (90 cm)
Finest seasonal colour	Summer blue Autumn golden yellow
Flower colour & timing	Golden-bronze, August–September
Growing conditions	Sun; ordinary garden conditions to dry
Landscape use	Single, naturalizing; flower arrangements
Growth habit	Clumping

Spartina pectinata 'Aureomarginata'
(prairie cord grass)

Pronunciation	spar-TEE-nah pek-tin-AH-tah
Zone	4–7
Form	Tall, upright arching
Size	Foliage 3' (90 cm) Flower 5' (1.5 m) Width 3' (90 cm)
Finest seasonal colour	Summer yellow variegated
Flower colour & timing	Golden, August–September
Growing conditions	Sun; ordinary garden conditions
Landscape use	Single, mass planting, naturalizing
Growth habit	Moderately invasive

grasses at a glance

Sporobolus heterolepis	
(prairie dropseed)	
Pronunciation	spor-AH-bol-us het-er-oh-LEP-is
Zone	4–8
Form	Medium, arching
Size	Foliage 1' (30 cm) Flower 2' (60 cm) Width 2' (60 cm)
Finest seasonal colour	Autumn bronze
Flower colour & timing	Scented bronze, August
Growing conditions	Sun; ordinary garden conditions
Landscape use	Single, mass planting, naturalizing
Growth habit	Clumping

Stipa tenuissima	
(Mexican feather grass)	
Pronunciation	STYE-pah ten-yoo-ISS-ih-mah
Zone	6–10
Form	Medium, arching
Size	Foliage 1' (30 cm) Flower 2' (60 cm) Width 1' (30 cm)
Finest seasonal colour	Summer light green
Flower colour & timing	White, July
Growing conditions	Sun; ordinary garden conditions
Landscape use	Single, mass planting, naturalizing
Growth habit	Clumping

selected reading

Baker, Mary E. F. *The Book of Grasses.* Garden City: Doubleday, 1912.

Brooklyn Botanic Garden Record. *Plants & Gardens: Ornamental Grasses.* Brooklyn: Brooklyn Botanic Garden, Inc., 1988.

Brookes, John. *The Book of Garden Design.* New York: Macmillan, 1991

Darke, Rick. *For Your Garden: Ornamental Grasses.* Toronto: Little, Brown & Co., 1994.

Darke, Rick. *The Colour Encyclopedia of Ornamental Grasses.* Portland, OR: Timber Press, 1999.

Greenlee, John. *The Encyclopedia of Ornamental Grasses.* New York: Michael Friedman Publishing Group, Inc., 1992.

Hawley, Patricia. *Grasses.* Aylesbury, Bucks, UK: Shire Publications, 1989.

Jekyll, Gertrude. *Colour Schemes for the Garden.* (Reprint) Antique Collectors' Club, 1982.

Johnson, Lorraine. *The Ontario Naturalized Garden: The Complete Guide to Using Native Plants.* North Vancouver: Whitecap Books, 1995.

King, Michael and Piet Oudolf. *Gardening with Grasses.* Portland, OR: Timber Press, 1998.

Macself, Albert James. *Grass.* London: Cecil Palmer, 1924.

Madson, John. *Where The Sky Began: Land Of The Tallgrass Prairie.* Boston: Houghton Mifflin Company, 1982.

Oakes, A.J. *Ornamental Grasses and Grasslike Plants.* Scarborough, ON: Nelson Canada, 1990.

Oudolf, Piet with Noël Kingsbury. *Designing with Plants.* Portland, OR: Timber Press, 1999.

Reinhardt, Thomas, Marina Reinhardt, and Mark Moscowitz. *Ornamental Grass Gardening: Design Idea, Functions and Effects.* New York: Michael Friedman Publishing Group, 1994.

Taylor, Nigel J. *Ornamental Grasses, Bamboos, Rushes & Sedges.* New York: Sterling Publishing Co., 1992.

index

*Grasses listed appear in illustrations or photographs

First published in Canada in 2003 by Whitecap Books Ltd.

This edition published in the United States by
Ball Publishing
335 N. River St.
PO Box 9
Batavia, Illinois 60510
www.ballpublishing.com

Edited Elaine Jones
Proofread Lesley Cameron
Cover design Roberta Batchelor
Interior design Stacey Noyes / LuzForm Design
Photographs Martin Quinn
Illustrations Wendy Hogenbirk

Printed and bound by Imago in Singapore

10   09   08   07   06   05   04   1   2   3   4   5   6   7   8

The Cataloging-in-Publication data for this title is available from the Library of Congress.